Conservatism

in America

VARIETIES OF *Conservatism* IN AMERICA

Edited by

PETER
BERKOWITZ

Contributors

RANDY E. BARNETT

JOSEPH BOTTUM

RICHARD A. EPSTEIN

JACOB HEILBRUNN

MARK C. HENRIE

TOD LINDBERG

HOOVER
INSTITUTION
PRESS
Stanford University
Stanford, California

www.hoover.org

Hoover Institution Press Publication No. 533

First printing, 2004
11   10   09   08   07   06   05   04   9   8   7   6   5   4   3   2   1

Manufactured in the United States of America

The paper used in this publication meets the minimum requirements
of the American National Standard for Information Sciences—
Permanence of Paper for Printed Library Materials, ANSI Z39.48-1992.

Library of Congress Cataloging-in-Publication Data

Varieties of conservatism in America / edited by Peter Berkowitz.
        p.   cm. — (Hoover Institution Press publication series ; 533)
    Includes bibliographical references and index.
    ISBN 0-8179-4572-5
    1. Conservatism—United States.   I. Berkowitz, Peter, 1959–
II. Series: Hoover Institution publication ; 533.
JC573.2.U6V37   2004
320.52'0973—dc22   2004018281

CONTENTS

Randy E. Barnett is the Austin B. Fletcher Professor at Boston University School of Law. After graduating from Northwestern University and Harvard Law School, he served as a criminal prosecutor in Chicago. His areas of scholarship include constitutional law, contract law, criminal justice, political theory, and jurisprudence. He is the author of *The Structure of Liberty: Justice and the Rule of Law* (Clarendon Press, 1998) and *Restoring the Lost Constitution: The Presumption of Liberty* (Princeton University Press, 2004).

Peter Berkowitz teaches at George Mason University School of Law and is a fellow at the Hoover Institution, Stanford University. He is a founding codirector of the Jerusalem Program on Constitutional Government and served as a senior consultant to the President's Council on Bioethics. He is the author of *Virtue and the Making of Modern Liberalism* (Princeton University Press, 1999) and *Nietzsche: The Ethics of an Immoralist* (Harvard University Press, 1995), as well as the editor of *Never a Matter of Indifference: Sustaining Virtue in a Free Republic* (Hoover Institution Press, 2003) and of the companion to this volume, *Varieties of Progressivism in America* (Hoover Institution Press, 2004). He has written on a variety of topics for a variety of newspapers, magazines, and journals.

Joseph Bottum is books and arts editor of the *Weekly Standard*, poetry editor of *First Things*, and author of *The Fall & Other Poems*.

Richard A. Epstein is the James Parker Hall Distinguished Service Professor of Law at the University of Chicago, where he has taught since 1972. In addition, he has been the Peter and Kirstin Bedford Senior Fellow at the Hoover Institution since 2000. He has been a member of the American Academy of Arts and Sciences since 1985 and a senior fellow of the Center for Clinical Medical Ethics at the University of Chicago Medical School since 1983. His books include *Skepticism and Freedom: A Modern Case for Classical Liberalism* (University of Chicago, 2003); *Cases and Materials on Torts*, 8th edition (Aspen Law & Business, 2004); *Torts* (Aspen Law & Business, 1999); *Principles for a Free Society: Reconciling Individual Liberty With the Common Good* (Perseus Books, 1998); *Mortal Peril: Our Inalienable Rights to Health Care?* (Addison Wesley, 1997); *Simple Rules for a Complex World* (Harvard, 1995); *Bargaining With the State* (Princeton, 1993); *Forbidden Grounds: The Case Against Employment Discrimination Laws* (Harvard, 1992); *Takings: Private Property and the Power of Eminent Domain* (Harvard, 1985); and *Modern Products Liability Law* (Greenwood Press, 1980).

Jacob Heilbrunn is an editorial writer for the *Los Angeles Times*. He was previously a senior editor at the *New Republic*. He was a 1994 Arthur F. Burns fellow and a 1998 Japan Society fellow. He is currently writing a book on neoconservatism for Doubleday.

Mark C. Henrie is senior editor of the Intercollegiate Studies Institute in Wilmington, Delaware. He is the author of *A Student's Guide to the Core Curriculum* (ISI Books, 2000) and editor of *Doomed Bourgeois in Love: Essays on the Films of Whit Stillman* (ISI Books, 2001).

Tod Lindberg is a research fellow at the Hoover Institution, Stanford University. He is editor of *Policy Review*, Hoover's Washington, D.C.–based bimonthly journal. He writes a weekly column about politics for the *Washington Times* and is a contributing editor to the *Weekly Standard*. He is the editor of the forthcoming *Beyond Paradise and Power: Europe, America, and the Future of a Troubled Partnership* (Routledge, 2004).

ACKNOWLEDGMENTS

This book and its companion volume, *Varieties of Progressivism in America*, appear under the auspices of the Hoover Institution's Initiative on American Individualism and Values. Both volumes are animated by the conviction that it is advantageous, particularly at this moment of high partisan passion in the United States, to explore the inclinations, opinions, and ideas that inform partisan differences, as well as the principles that partisans in America share. The volumes, and the conviction that animates them, have enjoyed the generous support of Hoover Institution director John Raisian and deputy director David Brady.

INTRODUCTION

Peter Berkowitz

THE INTENSE PARTISAN strife of the past several years has impeded understanding of the hard choices ahead. By suggesting that for every issue, at home and abroad, we must choose between two bitterly antagonistic and utterly irreconcilable alternatives, the polarization of our politics obscures the critical differences and distinctions within, as well as the important continuities that link, Left and Right in America. This book challenges the reductionist tendencies of the moment by bringing into focus the varieties of conservatism in America. Its companion volume, *Varieties of Progressivism in America,* addresses the same challenge but on the other side of the political spectrum.

Whereas to many critics all conservatives look alike, conservatives themselves disagree, sometimes sharply, about what it means to be a conservative and who is entitled to bear the name. To be sure, all conservatives agree that it means committment to conserving moral and political goods that are in danger of being lost or degraded. But which goods? Is it traditional morality and religion that conservatives seek to conserve? Or is it rather the basic legal framework of a free society? Or is it the manners, mores, and principles of a self-governing

people? And what are the most pressing dangers to which the American political order gives rise? The quest for unfettered personal autonomy? The trampling of rights of property and contract? The
consumption of the moral capital on which freedom depends? These
are the questions that divide conservatives in America today. The
chapters in this book demonstrate the variety of answers put forward
by classical conservatives, libertarians, and neoconservatives.

The book's structure and style reinforce the conviction that conservatism in America represents a family of opinions and ideas rather
than a finished doctrine or a settled creed. For starters, our contributors are drawn from different professional backgrounds. Three are
editors at influential magazines of conservative opinion. Two are distinguished law professors. One writes editorials for a major daily news-
paper. Each brings his distinctive voice to bear. It was not a
requirement that they subscribe to the views that they were charged
with expounding, but in most cases they do and in all cases they have
sympathy for those views. Whereas the journalists among the contributors are unusual for their keen interest in ideas, the professors
stand out for their attention to the impact of ideas on practice. As a
result, all of the contributors are well-positioned to clarify the moral
underpinnings of the varieties of conservatism in America and to shed
light on the political implications of each variety.

Part I examines classical conservatism. According to Mark Henrie,
the "traditionalist" strand is, paradoxically, of relatively recent vintage.
Born in the years following World War II, it represented a break with
the dominant forms of progressivism and conservatism in America,
both of which were conventionally liberal and maintain equality
before the law: they affirmed that the chief aim of politics was to
protect individual liberty but disagreed about the role of government
in redistributing wealth and regulating social and economic affairs. In
contrast, "the New Conservatism," developed most influentially by
Russell Kirk in *The Conservative Mind* (1953), emphasized the foundations of politics in natural law or transcendent moral order; the

authority of religion, particularly Christianity; the wisdom of inherited social forms; the dangers of innovation; and the limits of the scientific study of society. Under the aegis of liberalism, Kirk contended, Americans had lost an appreciation of human goods and the fullness of human nature. As an initial corrective, he advocated a revivification of the "moral imagination" through the study of great literature.

Traditionalist conservatives recognize the benefits of political freedom, Henrie observes, but they do not aim to save or correct the larger liberalism that undergirds American politics. Rather, their goal is to contain it, because in their view the liberal tradition falsely purports to provide the comprehensive and final account of the purposes of moral and political life. Accordingly, traditionalist public policy positions seek to create space for traditional alternatives within a liberal framework. For example, traditionalist conservatives prefer a policy toward the family that views marriage as the entering into a status rather than the striking of a contract. They favor educational policies that expand opportunities for parents to send their children to schools that openly teach religious values. They accept free markets as the right way to run an economy, criticizing the culture of dependency they believe is promoted by socialism and by the welfare state while increasingly also criticizing the culture of constant change and frenetic movement generated by globalizing capitalism. They are also skeptical of an interventionist foreign policy—in part because they demand a more direct and conventional connection between national interest and U.S. military action than the promotion of human rights and in part because they reject the understanding of America as embodying a universal liberalizing mission.

Joseph Bottum agrees with Henrie that paradox lies at the heart of conservatism in America. He contends that conservatism is an essentially modern phenomenon, arising in Europe in the late nineteenth century to preserve medieval political forms in reaction to the liberal and universalizing themes of the French Revolution. Yet in the

United States, conservatives must, in one form or another, seek to conserve the results of the American Revolution and, thus, the liberal and universalizing doctrine embodied in such founding documents as the Declaration of Independence and the Constitution. The "perpetual dilemma of modern conservatism," Bottum maintains, is that because modernity is, in significant measure, the history of the development of liberalism and because liberalism is essentially progressive in character, modern conservatism mainly consists of preserving a form of thought and life that seeks to release individuals from the authority of custom and tradition. So conservatives look for opportunities to preserve as much premodernity as is good for and consistent with modern liberalism.

For Bottum, the big question is whether conservatives can find ways to resist liberalism's tendency to turn liberty into license. What social conservatives understand, suggests Bottum, is that abortion is the test case. For Bottum believes that abortion represents license to kill. Indeed, he observes that the progressive imperatives to care for the vulnerable and to extend rights to those who lack them could justify liberal opposition to abortion and, for a time in the 1960s, seemed to require it for some then on the left. Yet over the past forty years, the liberal impulse to entrench and expand the claims of personal autonomy has compelled progressives to favor the personal freedom of women over the rights of the unborn. What permits this preference for one liberal imperative over another, according to Bottum, is a weakening of biblical religion in Americans, which once provided the moral frame of reference within which our liberal republic was created and which, for much of our history, served as an unspoken authority over and limitation upon the pursuit of happiness. Bottum traces a widening cultural divide between believers and secularists and contends that a growing array of issues—from the use of embryos for stem cell research and the propriety of same-sex marriage to the war in Iraq—reliably tracks the divisions over abortion. He concludes that the opposition to abortion is the ground on which different conservative camps have and should continue to come together.

Part II deals with libertarianism. According to Randy Barnett, the core of contemporary libertarianism is the belief that the preservation of individual liberty depends on the primacy of property rights, freedom of contract, and the free market. Libertarians tend to divide over whether property rights should be understood as strict moral imperatives or valued because of the good social consequences they produce. In Barnett's view, there is no need to choose. For one thing, most people are endowed with moral intuitions that support both reasoning about rights based on their moral necessity and reasoning about rights based on an appeal to the good social consequences that come from respecting them. Each form of reasoning provides a check on the other, identifying the limits beyond which one approach alone leads to absurd or unjust conclusions while often converging and thus providing support for the other. Yet even taken together, the two forms of reasoning about rights are inadequate to account for the full range of norms and principles on which our law is based. One must also take into account, insists Barnett, the set of beliefs and practices known as "the rule of law," in particular the judge-made common law that the United States inherited from England. This law provides formal procedures that impel judges to resolve real-world disputes by developing doctrines that tend to vindicate individual rights viewed both as moral imperatives and as devices for securing good social consequences.

The end toward which libertarians strive, the standard that permits them to judge any particular legal ruling or act of legislation as an improvement or as a mistake, is the classical liberal view of the rightly ordered political society. According to Barnett, such a society is based on the recognition that all persons are, by nature, free and equal; that government has no business prescribing a single conception of the good life; and that each person has the right to pursue happiness as he or she sees fit, limited only by the requirement of allowing a like liberty for others. To create the conditions for the maintenance of political order governed by these premises, the classical liberal tradition has expounded a catalog of rights—concerning acquisition and use of property, the making and enforcing of contracts, self-defense, and restitution for interference with the use and enjoyment of one's property—which it calls natural, regards as nonnegotiable or inalienable, and understands to create state-enforceable duties. Barnett stresses that there is more to moral and political life than these natural rights. However, he insists that what he calls the realm of natural law ethics, which concerns moral virtue and the good life, lies beyond the province of libertarian thought. Libertarians are by no means indifferent to this realm; however, they do believe that government should, in general, stay neutral toward those competing conceptions of the good life that are consistent with respect for the rights of others but should oppose those that aren't.

Complementing Barnett's focus on the theoretical foundations of libertarianism, Richard Epstein surveys the basic elements of a libertarian legal framework and shows the salutary effects they have on character. In offering this analysis, Epstein deliberately elides the important differences between strict libertarian thought and classical liberalism—namely, that the latter allows for the use of taxation and eminent domain, which offends strict libertarian premises. Even with that caveat, Epstein is well aware that his undertaking cuts against the grain: as Barnett indicated, broadly conceived, libertarian thought typically restricts itself to establishing the limits of the coercion the state can legitimately use against individuals and to setting rules that most think of as moral minimums. But Epstein makes a sociological point: the legal rules that govern everyday life inevitably exert a powerful influence on character, creating incentives to behave in ways that the system rewards and selecting for those who are well-endowed with the traits the legal system values. Although he insists that there is a great deal more to the education of character than the legal organization of society, Epstein argues that libertarian-based legal rules, especially in contrast to welfarist or redistributivist rules, produce virtues in citizens that are both humanly attractive and conducive to the maintenance of a free society; thus, they provide further justification for a libertarian approach.

So, for example, the libertarian view that each person should keep what he earns because he is the owner of his own labor encourages industry and productivity. The libertarian position that the first possessor of property owns it to the exclusion of all others rewards those who are quick to spot opportunities and profit from them, not necessarily only to their own advantage but also to the advantage of family, friends, and society as a whole. The libertarian stress on a strict interpretation of the law of contract creates strong incentives for individuals to develop reputations for reliability and competence. And a regime that vigorously protects property rights and enforces contracts for the mutually agreed upon exchange of property encourages the arts of compromise, negotiation, and cooperation. Moreover, by limiting the actionable causes of harm to the punishment of aggression and deceit, rather than extending them to harms suffered from losses in the labor market or personal offenses stemming from the private conduct of others, a libertarian-informed tort system motivates people to concentrate on increasing their own competence and productivity. In sum, Epstein contends that the libertarian framework is preferable not only because it safeguards essential rights and produces economic prosperity but also because of the sound human character it forms.

Part III explores neoconservatism. As Jacob Heilbrunn observes in an essay concentrating on foreign policy, neoconservatism, about which one heard little in the 1990s, has been thrown back into the spotlight by the war in Iraq and the effort to establish order and democracy in the aftermath of the liberation of Baghdad. Critics on both left and right have been vociferous in contending that the war was hatched as a neoconservative conspiracy and that our mistakes in carrying it out derive from neoconservative proclivities. Heilbrunn disagrees, suggesting instead that where matters have gone wrong is in proceeding too little as neoconservatism would dictate, sending too few troops to defeat all of Saddam's forces, and bringing to bear too few resources to democratize Iraq speedily. More generally, Heilbrunn inclines to Irving Kristol's opinion that the historical mission of neoconservatism has been to convert the "Republican party, and American conservatism in general, against their respective wills, into a new kind of conservative politics suitable to governing a modern democracy." In the field of foreign policy, this has meant, in contrast to both the "crabbed amoralism" of conservative realists and the squeamish idealism of progressive multilateralists, firm opposition to totalitarianism coupled with strong support for the energetic use of the American military to promote democracy abroad.

Heilbrunn makes his case by tracing the historical arc of neoconservative thought. Although he dismisses the charge that neoconservatism reflects Leninist or Trotskyist ambitions to bring about utopia at any cost, he nevertheless argues that the roots of neoconservatism lie in the ideological battles over communism of the 1930s. And although sympathetic to the Socialist critique of capitalism, the founders of neoconservatism were solidly opposed to both the Soviet Union and Stalin. Indeed, according to Heilbrunn, their passionate opposition to Stalinism led them to underestimate the evil of Nazism in the early 1940s and to go gentle on Senator Joseph McCarthy in the early 1950s. Heilbrunn contends that the extent to which the original neoconservatives turned rightward in response to the rise of the New Left and to student unrest on campuses across the country during the 1960s has been exaggerated. He insists that neoconservative sensibility had always been wary of the weaknesses of liberalism—particularly in its softness toward the radical left—and alert to the excesses that it spawned. In the 1970s, neoconservatives came into their own as a political force. Opposing both McGovernite reluctance to the use of force and Kissingerian willingness to do business with dictators, they rallied around the progressive hawk, Democratic senator Henry "Scoop" Jackson. In the 1980s, they embraced Ronald Reagan to the hilt. In the 1990s, they fully supported President Bill Clinton's interventions in Bosnia and Kosovo. Since September 11, 2001, they have provided intellectual firepower, inside and outside the Bush administration, for aggressively prosecuting the war on Islamic extremism by removing Saddam Hussein from power and seeking to implant democracy in the Arab Middle East. And they have come in for heavy criticism for the unanticipated challenges of rebuilding Iraq.

Although Tod Lindberg concentrates on the future of neoconservatism, he begins with the origins of politics in competing interests and differences of opinions and sentiment. Given these stubborn realities, liberal democracy, he contends, reflects the form of political life most adequate to our nature as free and equal persons. Thus, he is in agreement with Mark Henrie and Joseph Bottum that, in contrast to classical conservatives, neoconservatives aim to conserve liberalism because they believe it is the best form of political life. Lindberg is also in agreement with Jacob Heilbrunn that neoconservatives see a convergence between national interest and moral imperative in the promotion of liberal democracy abroad. What particularly distinguishes neoconservatives, according to Lindberg, is the acute awareness of the dangers to a liberal order that come from within liberalism itself. This is not to say that liberalism carries the seeds of its own destruction, Lindberg stresses. For liberalism came well equipped with self-correcting powers. In Lindberg's view, the special contribution of the neoconservatives to the understanding of liberalism is to appreciate that balancing the often competing claims of freedom and equality is the great and unending political task in a liberal democracy.

According to Lindberg, neoconservatism has, over the past several decades, promoted a more balanced approach to the challenges of liberal democracy in America in four ways. First, what Lindberg calls the "neoconservative turn" of the 1960s introduced a heavy dose of realism into public debate in America by demanding that law and policy be evaluated in light of the actual outcomes they produced rather than on the basis of the worthiness of the intentions that motivated, or the elegance of the theory that generated, them. Second, the neoconservative critique of the moral foundations of capitalism, although initially sounding the alarm that the free market system was drawing down the moral capital on which it depended, helped reveal the internal resources that capitalism, and by extension liberal democracy itself, has for correcting and sustaining itself. Third, neoconservative foreign policy, particularly in its resolute opposition to communism, sought to combine a tough-minded realist appreciation of the role of nations' narrow self-interest in international relations with an insistence that liberal democracy was morally superior to all competitors and that American military power made the world a generally safer and more stable place. And fourth, neoconservatives stressed that America's particular virtues were indissolubly connected to liberalism's universal claims and that America's peace and prosperity were inseparable from the spread of liberal democracy abroad. To appreciate that such balancing is the very essence of politics in a liberal democracy, concludes Lindberg, is a sign of progress and a precondition for conserving freedom and equality under law.

The debate among conservatives about which principles and practices are most urgently in need of protection continues. The essays in this volume demonstrate that it is in significant measure a debate with that larger liberalism that undergirds the American constitutional order. The essays also suggest that this larger liberalism, with its bedrock devotion to individual liberty and equality before the law, serves as the common ground on which the contending camps within conservatism—and indeed conservatives in their contentions with progressives—can come together, debate civilly, and discover ways to advance the public good.

Classical Conservatism

CHAPTER ONE

Understanding Traditionalist Conservatism

Mark C. Henrie

IN THE YEARS following the Second World War, a group of writers emerged who became known as America's New Conservatives, prominently including Richard M. Weaver, Peter Viereck, Robert Nisbet, and Russell Kirk.[1] In this case, "new" did not merely indicate a generational transition; these thinkers did not represent a simple return to the conservatism of the 1930s following the emergency of world war. Instead, the New Conservatives articulated ideas and concepts that were virtually unprecedented in American intellectual history. They took their political bearings from a quite novel set of intellectual authorities. Most striking of all, at the very moment of America's historic victory over the most potent totalitarian threat of the century, their writings were redolent with sometimes sweeping doubts about

1. See Richard M. Weaver, *Ideas Have Consequences* (Chicago: University of Chicago Press, 1948); Peter Viereck, *Conservatism Revisited: The Revolt Against Revolt, 1815–1949* (New York: Charles Scribner, 1949); Robert Nisbet, *The Quest for Community: A Study in the Ethics of Order and Freedom* (New York: Oxford University Press, 1953); and Russell Kirk, *The Conservative Mind: From Burke to Santayana* (Chicago: Henry Regnery, 1953).

the "progress" of the Modern Project—and about the individualism at the heart of modern liberalism's liberty.

Central to the conservatism of the 1930s was intransigent opposition, on the part of various Republican-leaning social groups, to the "socialism" of Franklin Roosevelt's New Deal. The possessing classes resisted state-directed bureaucratic administration of the economy in the name of an older form of liberal capitalist social order. Among intellectuals, articulate conservatism in the 1930s was represented by such men as H. L. Mencken, George Santayana, Irving Babbitt, and Albert Jay Nock.[2] With the partial exception of Santayana, each may be said to have subscribed to a version of classical liberalism or libertarianism that emphasized something resembling John Stuart Mill's individuality, as opposed to social conformity. Without exception, their worldviews were markedly elitist and sharpened by religious skepticism. This last could be seen in Santayana's genteel atheism, in Mencken's noisy contempt for American Bible-thumpers, in Nock's preference for the most coldly rationalist of French freethinkers, and in Babbitt's quest for wisdom in Hinduism after dismissing his Puritan ancestry. In other words, these prewar conservatives connected not at all with the lived traditions of the vast majority of the American people, except on the single point of the tradition of individualism, whether rugged or not.

Kirk, of course, quickly became the leading figure of the New Conservatism—a position that later received the appellation of "traditionalism" or "traditionalist conservatism." It was also referred to as "Burkean conservatism," after the British statesman and writer Edmund Burke (1729–1797). Burke had long been recognized as the font of British and some strands of continental European conservatism, but his influence in America was generally held to be negligible. Although Kirk himself was influenced by some of the currents of thought in the 1930s, and though *The Conservative Mind* purported

2. See Robert Crunden, ed., *The Superfluous Men: Critics of American Culture, 1900–1945* (Wilmington: ISI Books, 1999).

to be a "recovery" of a preexisting Burkean tradition in American political and social thought, it is difficult to deny that there was also a large element of invention in Kirk's account of the conservative tradition. Kirk's "canons" of conservatism began with an orientation to "transcendent order" or "natural law"—a view that political problems are, at bottom, religious and moral problems rather than the other way around. Whereas the libertarian conservatives of the 1930s usually understood themselves as heirs of various enlightenment dissenters from Europe's Christian civilization, Kirk was a dissenter from the tradition of dissent, striving to learn from the sidelined champions of orthodox religion. Kirk therefore rejected rationalism, utilitarianism, and egalitarianism. He tied freedom to property holding, but there is no discussion of the "magic of the marketplace" or interest in economic efficiency. He was hostile to the experimentalism of the social scientific mind, and he defended the latent reasonableness of evolved social forms. The three evils that emerge as antagonists throughout *The Conservative Mind* are the French Revolution, the Industrial Revolution, and the bureaucratic-managerial revolution of the first half of the twentieth century. Communism is mentioned hardly at all.

Focusing on the French Revolution, Kirk stated emphatically that the overarching evil of the age was "ideology," and he claimed that conservatism, properly understood, is "the negation of ideology." As such, conservatism prescribes a "politics of prudence," a cautious statesmanship founded upon a sensitive understanding of the complexities of *human nature*, the limitations of human history, and the capaciousness of the human good. Of course, liberalism's ancient boast has always been that it founds itself upon, and best adequates to, *human nature*—once that nature is shorn of illusions and superstition. From the point of view of the liberal mind, one might even say that if ideology were defined as a project for achieving a utopian intellectual abstraction, then it is liberalism that is the negation of ideology.

From Kirk's perspective, there is a partial truth in liberalism's claims: liberty is a genuine element of the human good, and individual human beings are worthy of a respect that is roughly, imperfectly realized in the liberal doctrine of rights. Consequently, Kirk could find significant areas of common ground with classical liberals such as F. A. Hayek (while forcefully eschewing more doctrinaire libertarians) and, up to a point, with the chastened liberals we now know as neoconservatives. But to Kirk, and to the American traditionalists he inspired, liberals ultimately fail to understand the partiality of their core principle. Their account of human nature excludes too much of what can be known, and is known, about the human good. Because their principle of individual liberty is "simple" or "reductionist," liberals possess no "other" principle that can authoritatively limit the eventual application of their principle to all spheres of human life—this despite their proud boast that liberalism differs in kind from all other political theories in refusing for itself a "comprehensive conception of the good." Because, for liberalism, the public sphere is limited only by rights, which are the possession only of those great abstractions, "individuals," the public sphere in fact extends to all human relations. The homogenization of the entire human world on the basis of the contract theory is the dehumanizing threat we ultimately face, made all the more dangerous by the fact that America's political discourse has lacked any terms that would enable us to recognize the ideological or dogmatic character of liberalism.

Consequently, Kirk's other great theme, repeated throughout his life, was an appeal to revivify the "moral imagination" through a serious engagement with poetry and imaginative literature. Such "romanticism" would seem to have little to do with the politics of prudence. However, this appeal was a recognition of, and a response to, the enveloping character of liberal presumptions in the thinking of all Americans. Alexis de Tocqueville had observed that censorship was unnecessary in America, because no American could imagine writing a book that would challenge the democratic regime. Kirk recognized the essential truth of Tocqueville's observation, but he considered this a stumbling block in the search for the whole truth about people rather than an indication that America was "the regime according to nature." Kirk's prophetic call for the cultivation of moral imagination was an attempt to free Americans from liberal ideology so that they could begin to *name* those "other" elements of the human good, which are obscured in the liberal dispensation.

Reaction to New Conservatism

Kirk's traditionalism quickly met with, and has long labored under, the accusation that it is, in effect, "un-American." The American tradition of political thought has always proceeded within the terms of the U.S. Constitution and the Federalist papers—evidently liberal documents. As Louis Hartz so famously argued, America is the Lockean country par excellence, with an aboriginal condition (or original position) closely resembling John Locke's state of nature and a founding compact reflecting Lockean principles. Consequently, there never has been, nor ever could be, a genuinely conservative party—in the European sense—in American life.[3]

Another important academic response to the New Conservatives was a 1957 article in the *American Political Science Review* by a young Samuel P. Huntington.[4] In attempting to come to terms with the quite unexpected emergence of a postwar American conservatism, Huntington engaged in an exercise in definition, considering three possible ways in which conservatism might be understood. The first alternative would be to follow the Marxist critique of ideologies. From such a perspective, ideologies would be superstructural rationalizations of the political power exercised in the basic struggle of socioeconomic classes. Emerging after the French Revolution's destruction of

3. Louis Hartz, *The Liberal Tradition in America* (New York: Harcourt, Brace, 1955).

4. Samuel P. Huntington, "Conservatism as an Ideology," *APSR* LI (June 1957): 454–73.

Europe's ancien régime, conservatism would then be the apologia for
the rule of the feudal nobility. Because there was no feudal class in
America's thoroughly bourgeois history, yet there were self-described
American conservatives in the 1950s, this "aristocratic" account of
American conservatism was unpersuasive.

Second, Huntington considered whether conservatism might be
understood as an "autonomous" body of ideas, in some sense a political theory on a par with liberalism or socialism or Marxism. Kirk's
list of conservative canons was duly noted, but Huntington dismissed
these, for he believed the range of ideas brought together in *The
Conservative Mind* was too diverse to form a coherent philosophy in
any way analogous to the "great" (or academically respectable) ideologies. Of course, as we have seen, Kirk himself would not have
disagreed with the contention that conservatism is not a member of
the genus, modern ideology. But whether, by that fact, conservatism
relinquishes all claim to an "autonomous" grounding of its ideas is
another matter.

Finally, Huntington settled on a "positional" understanding of
conservatism—an attitude toward change that endeavors to defend
the institutional status quo, whatever the status quo may be. Conservatism "properly understood" would thus emphasize organic development and guard against the revolutionary transformation of any
given regime. Such a conservatism would be legitimately Burkean, at
least with regard to process if not principles. In America, authentic
conservatism would be the conservation and consolidation of the progressive liberal tradition; Adlai Stevenson might serve as the exemplar
of such a conservatism. Anything else would be "reactionary" and,
thus, "un-American." In many ways, contemporary neoconservatives
occupy the role that Huntington prescribed for American conservatives. His critique of any political tendency "more" conservative than
this has been reprised by contemporary neoconservatives as well. Most
recently, Adam Wolfson intimated, with sensitivity and generous

regard, that Kirkian traditionalists wander dangerously close to un-American activities.[5]

But as we have seen rather pointedly, by placing Kirk in contrast to the prewar libertarian conservatives, there are several ways in which he was actually quite close to the values and aspirations of common Americans untutored in political theory. Today's traditionalist conservatives continue to be closer to many ordinary Americans on religious and moral matters—and on what we might call the "national question"—than are either libertarians or neoconservatives. Traditionalists can be understood as "un-American" only when America is understood definitively as the abstract embodiment of liberal theory. A younger Samuel Huntington thought in such terms.[6] But behold—with his latest book, *Who Are We?*, it would appear that Huntington himself has matured—into a traditionalist.[7]

Moral Sources

In a recent article in *The Public Interest*, Wolfson observed that traditionalists are animated by wistful memories of "an America of small towns and close-knit communities." He suggested that while such nostalgia may be charming, there is something fundamentally unreal or impracticable in the traditionalist worldview: we are all cosmopolites now. Norman Podhoretz, another neoconservative author, once boasted that what neoconservatism had signally added to an otherwise philistine American conservatism was a concern for *culture*. When it was pointed out to him that the writers of the traditionalist pantheon were, to a man, concerned with cultural questions above all else, his response was that the traditionalists were concerned with the wrong

5. Adam Wolfson, "Conservatives and Neoconservatives," *The Public Interest* 154 (Winter 2004): 32–48.

6. Samuel P. Huntington, *American Politics: The Promise of Disharmony* (Cambridge, MA: Belknap Press, 1981).

7. Samuel P. Huntington, *Who Are We? The Challenges to America's National Identity* (New York: Simon & Schuster, 2004).

sort of culture: they championed anachronistic, vaguely aristocratic litterateurs who were critical of modern democracy, whereas what was needed was attention to the cultural supporters of America's bourgeois order.[8] Claims concerning "historical availability" are prominent in neoconservative criticism of traditionalism.

Both these objections to traditionalist conservatism help illuminate a significant point of disagreement. In his article, Wolfson claimed Tocqueville as the neoconservative patron, in contrast to the traditionalists' Burke. But most traditionalists would contest this claim, wanting to view Tocqueville as one of their own, as Kirk himself did by including the Frenchman in his genealogy of the Anglo-American Burkean tradition. After all, Tocqueville viewed the emergent modern regime with distinctly mixed feelings, and he sought to *mitigate* democracy through the preservation and cultivation of "aristocratic" inheritances. One such inheritance in America is local government ("small towns and close-knit communities"); another is the "aristocratic" education of American lawyers, who appear to occupy a position not unlike that of the old *noblesse de robe*. Among the other "aristocratic" inheritances that Tocqueville sought to foster in America are the family and the Christian religion.

Wolfson maintained that in the collapse of ancient opinions and rules of life, "neoconservatives seek democratic substitutes for these older modes of living." While Tocqueville did advert to the democratic "substitutes" Americans had deployed in the absence of aristocratic inheritances—notably, of course, the associations—he did not preemptively presume that ancient rules of life were untenable at the first questioning. And while Tocqueville appears to have recognized the superior justice of modern democracy in comparison with older forms of political rule, one must be blind not to see his sense of sorrow at the loss of the human goods known in "aristocracy." In

8. Norman Podhoretz, "Neoconservatism: A Eulogy," *Commentary* 101, no. 3 (March 1996): 19–27; and Podhoretz's response to letters, *Commentary* 101, no. 6 (June 1996): 16.

fact, Tocqueville's peculiarly expansive definition of aristocracy as the universal form of premodern life, in contrast to the modern regime of popular sovereignty or democratic consent, constitutes a theoretical foundation for the universal or "autonomous" character of traditionalist conservatism—contra the young Samuel Huntington.

The traditionalist conservative's first feeling, the intuition that constitutes his or her moral source, is the sense of *loss*, and hence, of *nostalgia*. Those who are secure in the enjoyment of their own are often progressives of a sort, so confident in the solidity of their estate that they do not shrink from experimenting with new modes and orders. This was true, for example, of the French nobility of the ancien régime, who were often avid readers of the democratic theories of the philosophes and who, in practice, rejected their traditional patrimonial duties for the novelties of the court. This was true also of the planter class of the antebellum South, at least in the 1840s. Their writings are filled with an exuberant modernity. The conservative spirit, as such, arises only when loss is at hand or, probably more frequently, when loss has occurred. Consequently, there is always a "reactionary" dimension to such conservatism; the conservative typically arrives "too late" for mere conservation.

While in possession, we take our good for granted and thus often fail to recognize it. But in the face of loss, the human good is vividly revealed to us. We lament the loss of goods, not the loss of evils, which is why lament *illuminates*. Is it not striking that whereas antebellum Southern writers championed both the economic and moral superiority of the "peculiar institution," postbellum Southern conservatives typically did not *lament* the loss of slavery? Rather, the latter lamented the loss of gentility, gallantry, domesticity, and the virtues of yeoman agriculturalists. Although it may be true that nostalgia views the past through rose-colored glasses, such a criticism misses the point. To see the good while blinkered against evils is, nevertheless, *to see the good*. This is a source of knowledge, as well as a moral source; and here we may begin to glimpse facets of the human good beyond social functionality or mere utility, beyond all our theorizing.

So drenched in the progressive spirit is American political discourse (how could it be otherwise in the *novus ordo seclorum*?) that the backward glance is usually rejected out of hand and with the most facile of arguments. Ever since Burke's solicitous phrases about "Gothick" and "monkish" traditions, traditionalist conservatives have notably looked to the Middle Ages as a source of inspiration.[9] In doing so, one is met with a rejoinder of the sort, "But would you really want to live in an age before modern dentistry?" Southern traditionalists who speak well of the antebellum South almost always stand accused of being racist defenders of slavery. But why should such rejoinders count as definitive when the Modern Project, which is usually understood to have begun in the Renaissance, took as an inspiring model Athens—a society with no access to modern dentistry and built on a foundation of slave labor?

The point of this exercise in comparative nostalgia is not to score debater points but rather to achieve some clarity. Traditionalists do *not* wish to "turn back the clock" to premodern dentistry any more than the lovers of Periclean Athens wish to restore a slave economy. Polis-envy in the Renaissance and among some of our contemporaries serves as an indicator that a thinker is attracted to an ideal of political participation, as well as literary and philosophical originality and, perhaps, leisure, that he believes is unavailable or frustrated in the present. Traditionalist conservatives' kind words about medievalism indicate that they are attracted to forms of communal solidarity— loyalty and friendship, leisure, honor and nobility, and religious "enchantment"—that they believe are unavailable or frustrated in the present. As Tocqueville helped us understand, this list is not idiosyn-

---

9. It is important to observe that the French ancien régime existing immediately before the revolution was an innovative, and in many ways progressive, early-modern regime, not a medieval one. Consequently, at the time it seldom served as a conservative model—and almost never after the end of the Napoleonic period.

cratic; rather, it corresponds in its particulars to the deficits universally engendered by the modern regime.

For as conservative thinkers over the generations have intuited, and as Pierre Manent argued so persuasively in *An Intellectual History of Liberalism*,[10] the dominant political tradition of modernity did not simply discover a pattern laid up in heaven to contemplate. Rather, Enlightenment liberalism was a *project* that set out to transform the world. Moreover, this multigenerational project was aimed against a particular enemy—namely, the Church and, with it, the social world that Christianity had brought into being in Europe. Thus, the famous "state of nature" that grounds liberal argument is a cunning substitute for the biblical account of Eden. The bourgeois virtues of the commercial republic, in turn, are meant to supersede the classical and Christian virtues, which in some cases now assume the character of vices. The sovereignty of the people as the sole legitimating principle of the liberal regime places in question the sovereignty of God.

The construction of the modern liberal democratic regime has followed a circuitous path amid many, usually unacknowledged contingencies. In different times and places, the partisans of liberal progress have sided with enlightened monarchs, with parliaments, with executive agencies, and lately with constitutional courts. (Both Samuel Huntington and Stephen Holmes[11] objected that conservatives have defended so wide an array of institutions in various times and places that conservatism cannot be said to have a fixed or autonomous character. However, if conservatives have changed their defensive front over the decades, so too have liberals changed their mode of attack.) Still, there are permanent features to the world remade by Enlightenment, and conservative "medievalism" is a catalog of the consistent and pervading sense of *loss* brought on by the achievement of the

10. Pierre Manent, *An Intellectual History of Liberalism* (Princeton, NJ: Princeton University Press, 1994).

11. Stephen Holmes, *The Anatomy of Anti-Liberalism* (Cambridge, MA: Harvard University Press, 1993).

modern regime. Wherever there is a sense of loss, the conservative knows that there lies an indicator of some dimension of the human good.

From this discussion, we can discover something else about the traditionalist's "method." The philosophes cast doubt on the universal applicability of Christian "morals" in light of the diverse folkways of "natural men" whom European explorers had "discovered" (or claimed to have discovered) in their voyages. A common trope of the French Enlightenment was to question even the incest taboo as an unscientific "prejudice" of Christian civilization. But the Enlightened builders of the liberal regime were quite certain that they had discovered principles of political right that *were* universally applicable—and that in time might be applied beyond politics to the sphere of morals. Burke, in contrast, was guided by a kind of certainty in (traditional) morals, by an immediate intuition of the human good, while he viewed with the deepest skepticism speculative theories of political right. Whereas the Enlightenment "builds down" from politics to morals, the conservative "builds up" from morals to politics. Perhaps it would be fair to say that the liberal tradition, even today, has not yet generated a credible account of moral life. Perhaps it would be similarly fair to say that the conservative tradition has not yet generated a credible account of political life.

Boxing in Liberalism

Viewed in this way, it might be said that traditionalist conservatism is *not yet* a political theory but rather a tradition of social criticism that is working its way to a political philosophy adequate to its deepest moral intuitions. There is nothing extraordinary in such a view when we remember that the liberal tradition first reached something like a comprehensive theoretical articulation only in Locke, nearly two centuries after its moral rudiments came to light in the Renaissance and the Protestant Reformation. We are only little more than two centuries on from conservatism's birth in reaction to the French Revolution. Thus, the specifically *political* teaching of traditional conservatism remains provisional.

With this caveat in mind, one must nonetheless observe that traditionalist conservatism occupies a middle ground. On one side stand what we might call compleat liberals, who hold that some form of the principle of consent and the natural rights of individuals *is* justice, simply. What is more, justice so understood has primacy over all other dimensions of the human good. Any deviation from this principle is ipso facto illegitimate. Where hitherto held in abeyance, it must be pressed forward to completion. Anything—any human institution or rule of life—that we have hitherto valued that cannot stand under the conditions of liberal justice has no "right" to exist; the failure of any human institution when exposed to liberal principles is prima facie evidence of the prior existence of injustice in that institution. Thus, nothing genuinely just, and so nothing genuinely good, has been lost in the progress of the liberal regime: there is literally *no* cause for lament or nostalgia. "Let justice be done though the heavens fall." I take it that libertarianism is the compleat liberalism of the right.

On the other side are compleat reactionaries, such as Joseph de Maistre and Louis de Bonald, who entirely reject consent as a political and social principle and whose hatred for the modern regime knows no bounds.[12] The ancien régime must be restored in every particular, and there must be no concession on monarchic absolutism. As in the Garden of Eden, liberalism is grounded in a choice to traduce "the rights of God." Bonald's rallying cry was, in effect, "Monarchy, monotheism, monogamy: three great things that go great together." In the end, Maistre was driven to writing obscurantist hymns of praise for the joys of abject obedience, the salutary effects of human sacrifice,

---

12. Fascism, on this score, would not be continuous with Maistre and Bonald, because in various ways it was enamored of modern technology and actively endeavored to mobilize mass will, or the mass consent on the part of the people.

and the central role of the executioner in upholding civilized order. The great Tory Samuel Johnson, though far from a French retrograde, nonetheless could say with heartfelt vehemence, "The Devil was the first Whig." (And, indeed, must we not admit there is something of Milton's Satan in the liberal account of human virtues?)

It has long been conventional for political theorists to observe that Burke was, after all, a lifelong Whig. Because Locke was the political philosopher of the Whig settlement and the founder of the liberal tradition, Burke must be understood, in strong contrast to the continental reactionaries, as having no genuinely *fundamental* hostility to the modern regime. Perhaps, indeed, he might be thought of as the first neoconservative: if not a liberal, then at least a friend of liberalism. But as Kirk noticed in *The Conservative Mind*, Burke—in *Reflections* and afterward—"disavowed a great part of the principles of Locke." To take just one example, Burke deployed Lockean language about the contract of society only in an effort to explode that language's Lockean meaning. According to Kirk, conservatism after Burke owes "almost nothing" to Locke.[13]

I believe it is wrong, therefore, to understand the Burkean tradition as a sort of old-fashioned liberalism—or a sort of classical liberalism with some romantic doodads tacked on. It is also wrong to read the Burkean tradition in so strong a contrast to the continental retrogrades. If neoconservatives are aptly described as "conservative liberals"—as I believe they are—perhaps we can best understand the Burkean tradition as "liberal conservatism." Is this a distinction that makes a difference? I believe it does.

Liberal conservatism recognizes many of the *practical* advantages of liberalism, such as increased economic productivity and social peace. But in also recognizing the goods lost in the modern regime, such conservatism remains open to, and in search of, a revised *theo-*

13. Russell Kirk, *The Conservative Mind*, 7th ed. (Washington, DC: Regnery, 1953, 1995), 27.

retical account of political justice as such. Liberal conservatism does not reject the role of individual consent in politics, but nevertheless it retains a conviction that the human world cannot be wholly reconceived or reconstructed on that principle. Practically speaking, this means that liberal conservatives approach the notion of rights with great wariness, precisely because rights are "trumps." Characteristically, liberal conservatives tend to reify social institutions, seeing these institutions as possessing a species of subjectivity in their own right and, thus, not wholly comprehended by a term such as "voluntary association." The traditional common law is held in high esteem by liberal conservatives because its complex balancing of principles approaches rather closely to the whole truth about people; modern American jurisprudence is seen as a fantastic simplification of law to fit an ideological abstraction rather than real human beings.

Neoconservatism, or conservative liberalism, also occupies a middle ground. Unlike libertarians who aggressively seek to expand the principle of consent through all spheres of human interest, neoconservatives are the prudent or responsible liberals who understand that the tendency of liberal regimes to totalize their central principle constitutes a danger for the liberal regime itself. Neoconservatives admit that the liberal regime depends on a social capital that it does not itself generate. They therefore seek to restrain the liberal principle in select circumstances in the hope of "saving liberalism." But it is here that the conservative liberal and the liberal conservative part company. For it would appear, when all is said and done, that the neoconservatives are convinced that the liberal account of political right is in fact final and that their political activity is undertaken on liberalism's behalf. For the traditionalists, the question of political right remains open, and their political activity is undertaken to defend—for their own sake—human goods that are considered exogenous in liberalism. In other words, traditionalist conservatives endeavor to correct liberalism, not to save it. That is not to say that traditionalists yearn in any way for the "new gods" of postmodern paganism. Quite the contrary. The traditionalists' touchstones for the human good all lie in the past, not in some glorious visionary future. When confronted with the ideological monstrosities of our time, neoconservatives and traditional conservatives are certain allies. But until an account of political right appears that does justice to that which liberalism neglects, the traditionalist allegiance to the liberal regime remains decidedly grudging.[14]

Provisionally, therefore, one might describe the traditionalist conservative's political project as one of "containing liberalism" or of "boxing in" liberal justice. As the conservative movement in America crystalized in the 1950s and 1960s, a large, rather impressive, and quite understudied body of literature developed on the question of "tradition."[15] In retrospect, we can now see that "tradition" was a word deployed to indicate those moral contents of life that are eroded under liberalism; these studies were undertaken in an effort to understand the prerequisites for the persistence of those moral contents so that policies and jurisprudential concepts could be developed to safeguard those social structures in which the moral contents of life nat-

14. Paleoconservatives share with traditionalists the goal of seeking to supersede liberalism rather than to save it. But paleoconservatives may be distinguished from traditionalists to the extent that the former are unable to recognize any serious benefits in modernity and reject "mere nostalgia" while seeking to portray themselves as the vanguard of some future dispensation. If the goods of the modern regime prove incompatible with other human goods, compleat liberals effectively reject those other human goods in their wholehearted embrace of the regime of rights. For paleoconservatives, the reverse seems to be true: they effectively reject the goods of the modern regime in their wholehearted embrace of . . . something else. Traditionalist conservatives seek, instead, an account of political right that will conserve what is good in the modern regime while also returning to us the lost goods of the premodern dispensation.

15. See, for example, the essays in George W. Carey, ed., *Freedom and Virtue: The Conservative-Libertarian Debate* (Wilmington, DE: ISI Books, 1998, 2004). See also the first three volumes of Eric Voegelin's *Order and History* (Baton Rouge: Louisiana State Univerity Press, 1956), and Stanley Parry, "The Restoration of Tradition," *Modern Age* 5, no. 2 (Spring 1961): 125–38. Voegelin's work provided the most sophisticated philosophical approach to tradition for the postwar traditionalist conservatives.

urally arise. Emphasis was placed on "society" but not on what we know as "civil society." That is, emphasis was placed on elements of *Gemeinschaft* (organic community) rather than *Gesellschaft* (contractual society). Conservatives have sought to "make room," both conceptually and practically, for the flourishing of *Gemeinschaft*. Hence, the frequent invocation of Burke's "little platoons," as against the modern "grid" that reduces everything to the superintendence of the equal-protection state and the free market. Put another way, the political goal of traditional conservatism might be to keep the "public" realm small—but not in the liberal way, which makes the private (i.e., *individual*) realm large. What is wanted is a large and authoritative "social" realm.

Public Policy Today

The provisional nature of traditionalist conservatism's political principles and its wariness of "ideology" often lead to tentativeness in addressing disputed matters of public policy. There is also a strong element of "organicism" in conservative thought—as opposed, it is said, to "mechanistic" liberal social engineering. Gardening provides an apt metaphor for the traditionalist conservative's approach to statesmanship. Thus, such conservatives often act not so much to "achieve" certain ends but to create the conditions in which social goods may (or may not) flourish according to their nature. What is more, the traditionalist conservative appreciates that *all* political solutions are partial or temporary. There are no final solutions to the human predicament, and there will be no end of history.

The Family

Today, we often find that practical political advocacy reflecting a traditionalist perspective takes place in institutions that have the word "family" in their titles: Focus on the Family, the Family Research Council, various state-based think tanks such as the Pennsylvania

Family Institute, and the well-respected newsletter *Family in America*. Although many of these are relatively new institutions, traditionalist conservative concern about the family is not. In his "Letter to a Member of the National Assembly" (1791), Burke wrote: "As the relation between parents and children is the first among the elements of vulgar, natural morality . . . Your masters [the Jacobins] reject the duties of this vulgar relation, as contrary to liberty; as not founded in the social compact; and not binding according to the rights of men."[16] Burke had already seen that the cult of "rights" would be deployed *not* to shield citizens from obligations to the state; rather, rights would serve as an engine to break down the intermediate associational life of society, including even that primordial social building block, the family.

The contract tradition's reduction of human beings to autonomous individuals fosters a self-conception that destabilizes the marriage bond. The welfare state then "lubricates" exit from marriage with various substituting benefits. Love, it has been said, is the willingness to belong to another. There is little place for such love in a world of autonomous individuals bristling with rights—the world that liberalism understands as "natural." The popularity of a therapeutic language of "fulfillment" in contemporary America only exacerbates the weak institutional support that liberal jurisprudence provides for marriage. Traditional religious marriage ceremonies often included a prominent discussion of *sacrifice*, a concept that does not have ready appeal to autonomous individuals.

Traditionalist conservatives tend to see marriage as entering into a status rather than concluding a contract, and they would like to see this reflected in culture, law, and public policy. Thus, they look with approbation on movements, such as Promise Keepers, that work to shape popular culture in a family-friendly way. They would repeal the no-fault divorce revolution if they could—and, indeed, some Catholic

16. Edmund Burke, "A Letter to a Member of the National Assembly," in *Further Reflections on the Revolution in France*, ed. Daniel E. Ritchie, 50–51 (Indianapolis: Liberty Fund, 1992).

traditionalists would prefer the laws of marriage that prevailed until recently in several Latin American countries, where divorce was effectively impossible. The experiment with "covenant marriages" is viewed as a step forward, but a very small one. Traditionalists also favor shifting tax burdens from families to the single and childless. Again, George W. Bush's increased child tax credits are a small step forward.

Traditionalists believe that what liberalism views as "natural" is largely a fiction. They note that labor force participation by married women with children under age six is much lower than is commonly believed—about 60 percent, a sizeable percentage of which are only part-time. There is more of the "traditional family" intact in America, even at this late date, than the media typically report. Thus, traditionalists suggest that finding ways to support mothers of small children staying at home ought to be the norm for public policy rather than facilitating their return to the workplace. Traditionalist conservatives also favor repeal of various antidiscrimination laws that have rendered it illegal for businesses to recognize the differential burdens of (male) heads-of-households through the provision of a "family wage."[17]

The more hard-nosed traditionalists criticize those policies by which the welfare state comes to stand *in loco patris*, believing that husband-fathers would "naturally" be retrieved among the underclass in the absence of an alternative. There are even some who would entirely overhaul current law concerning child-support awards following divorce. The common law tended to tie the obligation of support to the right to control a child. The current near-universal practice, which grants mothers custody (control) and assigns fathers with financial obligations, yields precisely the opposite result.[18] Here again, the

17. See, for example, Allan Carlson, *From Cottage to Workstation: The Family's Search for Social Harmony in the Industrial Age* (San Francisco: Ignatius Press, 1993); and Allan Carlson, *The "American Way": Family and Community in the Shaping of the American Identity* (Wilmington, DE: ISI Books, 2003).

18. Stephen Baskerville illuminates this and other gory details of family law in

state comes to stand *in loco patris*, though it finances its role by gar-
nering a father's wages rather than through general taxation.

The currently controversial question of gay "marriage" is the
reductio ad absurdum of the liberal conception of marriage—marriage, as Kant put it, as a "contract for the mutual exercise of the
genitalia." But the bundle of legal "benefits" (and encumbrances) to
which gay couples say they seek access was never a recognition of
"love." Rather, these features of traditional marriage were accommodations to the "facts of life"—the fact that it is from the union of
one particular man and one particular woman that a new life arises,
together with a recognition that children are best reared to responsible
adulthood in the setting of a stable, well-capitalized, independent
household with a mother and a father. Marriage is *naturally* about
children.

Education

It is no accident that when liberalism attempts to think about marriage, it characteristically neglects the children. Children figure in the
state of nature of the proto-liberal Thomas Hobbes only as beings
that their begetters have chosen not to kill; nor are the "facts of life"
evident from the original position of the late-liberal John Rawls. In
the great premodern works of political philosophy, an educational
program for rearing the young was at the very heart of the account
of the res publica: education is emphatically a public matter. Indeed,
the proper education of the young was *the* political problem for both
Plato and Aristotle. But Locke's discussion of education takes place
in a separate treatise from his political work. Education must be considered a private matter if a regime of rights, of negative liberty, is to
be secured. Rather than a universal fact of human nature, the repro-
duction and rearing of children is viewed as an anomaly in the terms

---

contemporary America in his article "Is There Really a Fatherhood Crisis?" *Independent Review* 8, no. 4 (Spring 2004).

of social contract. Consequently, children are effectively relegated to an externality or assimilated to adult autonomy. What else is liberalism to do with such creatures who appear to be naturally dependent, naturally unequal, and naturally only potentially rational human beings, who naturally belong to their parents, who in turn naturally belong to them? In effect, liberalism must deny some of these essential facts or render them "unnatural," exceptions to the rule of individualism.

The absence of an educational doctrine cannot easily be remedied, however, because liberalism's boast is that it chastely denies to itself any thick theory of the good. Thus, it uniquely does not need to indoctrinate its citizens with controversial orthodoxies. But when the liberal state appropriated to itself the business of education with the advent of the "common school," it seized the responsibility of soul-craft—without really admitting to that fact. Education is, in its nature, value-laden. Liberalism's principled refusal to speak in teleological terms of a summum bonum, therefore, renders it a much-abashed patron of the schools. For, as every parent knows, children ask *Why?* and continue to ask *Why?* until they come to the end of the matter. A consistently liberal schooling must always stop short of that end, satisfying no one. For most of American history, the common schools surreptitiously reflected shared local values while the central organs of government looked the other way, a reasonable strategy for muddling through a theoretical inconsistency. Lately, however, courts have insisted on enforcing liberal norms on the schools, engendering a demoralization of society from the roots up. If, in the past, the schools stood in loco parentis, reflecting the values and exercising the discipline of parents in the domestic sphere, today the schools represent an ever-earlier exposure of children to the rights-bearing and market-choosing of the public sphere.

The traditionalist response has been to encourage experiments in alternatives of all kinds that might allow schools to reflect comprehensive conceptions of the good. A tuition tax credit was long the conservative goal, fostering the growth of an alternative, fully "private" (or, more properly, "social" or "domestic") system. Vouchers now seem a more politically feasible goal, though they also raise anxieties, since nothing yet has escaped the *control* that accompanies state "help."

Furthermore, traditionalists take hope from the burgeoning growth of home-schooling in our time. As recently as the 1980s, it stirred media comment when a home-schooler would gain admission to an elite university. Today, many university faculty report that their best students are usually the home-schoolers and that there are more of them each year. A cohort of well-mannered, morally serious, and intellectually curious young people is a gift to the country in its own right. But traditionalist conservatives also hope that as we absorb in our social imagination the fact of widespread home-schooling, we will begin to recognize something that was obscured by the progressive ideology of the common school—namely, that a public school is not an arrangement between the state and students but rather between the state and parents. Schools are best understood as providing one way (and not the only way) to serve, or even merely to supplement, the primarily *parental* office, which is simultaneously an obligation and a right, of educating one's own children.

Economics

Traditionalist conservatives have never made economics a principal area of inquiry. They have taken private property, market exchange, and the price mechanism all as something more or less natural, believing with Samuel Johnson that people are seldom so innocently employed as when they are making money. But traditionalists have advanced no particular doctrinal commitments, and they are sensitive to the artificial abstractions of modern corporate capitalism. During the second half of the twentieth century, traditionalist conservatives did oppose socialism, the growth of the welfare state, and most government regulation of the economy, but they did not necessarily do so for reasons of classical liberal political economy. Their primary concern was with the *culture* of socialism or of welfarism. In a similar way, many traditionalist conservatives today have begun to voice reservations about the *culture* of globalizing capitalism. Two cheers for capitalism is about right.

The economic theorist with the greatest appeal to the traditionalists has been Wilhelm Roepke, one of the founders of the classically liberal Mont Pelerin Society.[19] A German-Swiss Protestant, Roepke's work proceeded in dialogue with the Catholic social thought tradition, especially the papal encyclicals *Rerum Novarum* (1891) and *Quadragesimo Anno* (1931). Although fundamentally a defender of the free market, Roepke nonetheless embraced talk of a "third way" between socialism and capitalism. He warned of a kind of consumer materialism and social anomie arising from the totalizing reach of market "logic." He thus emphasized the need to embed the market amid strong social institutions and structures—boxing in liberalism in its economic dimension.

To box in the market would mean, first of all, to recognize that there are some things that should not be bought or sold, because to do so would directly violate human dignity or the common good. Thus, drugs, pornography, and prostitution are appropriately proscribed. So too, perhaps, certain biotechnologies. In a more speculative mode, religious traditionalists even raise questions about nursing homes and day care: ought *care* to be placed "on the market"? To embed market logic within a strong social setting also means to recognize human beings as something more than consumers. Thus, no one would disagree that Wal-Mart and free trade spell lower prices and often greater choice for Americans as consumers. But, to take the case of Wal-Mart, is not *something* lost, some kind of social capital, when the proprietors of a small town's chamber of commerce are

19. For a thoughtful introduction to Roepke's life and work, see John P. Zmirak, *Wilhelm Roepke: Swiss Localist, Global Economist* (Wilmington, DE: ISI Books, 2000).

"converted" into corporate employees? Is not something lost, as well as gained, in the proliferation of broadcast media? Is more choice always better? Does life in a consumer society perhaps promote superficial "lifestyles" structured by purchases and ephemeral fashions rather than "ways of life" structured by lasting commitments?

The limited liability corporation, of course, is one of the engines for economic growth in the modern world, a true prodigy of productivity. But is it not also something highly unnatural that exists only because it is artificially chartered and regulated by the state? There are no corporations in nature: they are fictitious legal persons. Unlike natural persons, they never grow old—which often limits a proprietor's access to new long-term capital—and they never die—which exacts from proprietary families a sizeable chunk of capital in inheritance tax. Proprietors may be motivated in their decisions by something beyond economic returns: by honorable standing or gratitude in the communities of their economic activity. Corporate management violates its fiduciary obligation to shareholders when it takes such matters into consideration. An economy dominated by the corporate form would seem to make all holders of capital into a version of the despised absentee landlords of old. What is more, the corporation is evidently more susceptible to implementing "politically correct" policies, whereas proprietary firms often exhibit more traditional domestic moral concerns. Withal, traditionalist conservatives have often written in favor of a widespread *distribution* of productive capital and in favor of smaller units of economic production. The question is not whether markets will be regulated; the question is what values shall structure that regulation.

Foreign Affairs

The first conservative literature on foreign affairs emerged from the French Revolution and the Napoleonic Wars. On the one hand, Burke can only be called an extremist in his rhetorically charged calls for Britain to destroy the Revolution altogether and to restore the

French ancien régime in every jot and tittle. On the other hand, we find, particularly among continental conservatives, numerous attempts to defend "variety" in regimes, with Maistre going so far as to describe each nation as willed by God in its particularity, each people (defined, for Maistre, linguistically) as possessing a particular providential mission. Consequently, continental conservatives sought to restore the traditional European balance of power. Faced with the ideological claims of a kind of political religion, the conservative responds with concerted action; but the conservative also knows that a society mobilized for war exacts a toll on domestic social structures that cannot easily be remedied. Because both Britain and America are "islands," they have been blessed historically with not needing large standing armies, with the state aggrandizement that these entail.

In the years immediately following victory in the Second World War, American conservatives, led by Senator Robert Taft, originally clamored to "bring the boys home"; whereas it was liberal Democrats who seemed intent on continuing America's global role. But minds were changed by growing awareness of the threat of Soviet communism. Communism was a universalist secular religion, a revolutionary movement recognizing no national boundaries. It was only the emergency of communism that convinced the majority of traditionalist conservatives that a highly interventionist foreign policy was required. Having become convinced, they were usually among the most hawkish of Cold Warriors.

However, during the post–Cold War "roaring nineties," the feelgood Clinton years of splendid irresponsibility, traditional conservatives were nearly united in their opposition to the wars for human rights in the Balkans. They considered that these military actions served no evident national interest. Traditionalist conservatives applauded President Bush's 2000 election rhetoric about a "humble" America in world affairs. They applauded the withdrawal from the Kyoto Treaty, which had, of course, never been presented to the Senate for ratification: withdrawal was interpreted as a signal that a "return to normalcy" was in the cards, following the long executive aggrandizement of the Cold War. Withdrawal from the Antiballistic Missile Treaty and the development of missile defense also seemed an admirably prudent long-term investment in national security.

Then came September 11, 2001. Traditionalist conservatives were again virtually united on the need to "take the fight" to al Qaeda in Afghanistan. But opinion became divided on the further military engagement in Iraq. Not least problematic was that, insofar as many traditionalists were religious believers, the Iraq war lacked an evident *causus belli*—an elementary requirement of just war doctrine. (And, indeed, the preemption doctrine articulated as America's official national strategy seems, at the level of theory at least, impossible to square with even quite permissive readings of the just war tradition.) Most traditionalists were nonetheless willing to support the war on the basis of the "clear and present danger" presented by weapons of mass destruction. Thus, the failure to discover such weapons in Iraq has proven a considerable blow.

Traditionalist conservative confidence in the Iraq policy has not been helped by the Bush administration's more recent embrace of muscular Wilsonian rhetoric as the justification for American actions. Woodrow Wilson is not a conservative icon. Sensitive to historical limitations and understanding liberal institutions as dependent on preexisting forms of social and cultural capital that are not present in Arab societies, traditionalists do not believe that "democracy"—which is to say, secular constitutional liberalism—is easily exported there. This does not mean that traditionalists do not take pride in America's having rid the world of Saddam Hussein's odious regime, nor does this mean that they now wish to cut our losses and withdraw. To abandon those Iraqis who have, at considerable risk to themselves, put their trust in us would be extremely dishonorable. To retreat, moreover, may well prove worse for American security in the long run. However, traditionalists would be reassured by a public rhetoric more closely tied to prudence and to the national interest.

The Wilsonian rhetoric of the Bush administration may reflect a calculation that it is in the nature of American society only to countenance foreign intervention when it is couched in messianic terms. But perhaps it would be easier for an American administration to transform American culture on this point than it is to transform, wholesale, the cultures of Arab societies far, far away.

Conclusion

The national narratives of most European peoples celebrate their moment of settlement into a particular place, an end to nomadic wandering, and the taking up of agriculture (and Christianity). It is striking that Americans celebrate not our settlement but rather our movement—setting off for the frontier. The liberal narrative of America as a "universal nation" corresponds to this unsettledness: to be a "universal" nation is precisely *not* to be a nation, a *gens*. Traditional conservatives have been endeavoring to *settle* America, to celebrate our arrival and not our departure, our actuality and not our potentiality, to bring Americans to see their national experience both as more particular than universal (which is to say, ideological) and as more in continuity with European precedents than in discontinuity; hence, Russell Kirk's determined effort to view the American War of Independence as "a revolution not made but prevented" and his Eurocentric account of "the roots of American order."

At this historical moment, with America incontestably the greatest power on Earth and with American popular culture driving all before it, such a project of self-limitation may seem a fantasy. And yet it was only yesterday evening, historically speaking, that the sun never set on the British Empire. Today, the captains and the kings have long departed. As that most eccentric of American thinkers, the nineteenth-century Catholic convert Orestes Brownson, observed,[20] the American

---

20. Orestes Brownson, *The American Republic* (Wilmington, DE: ISI Books, 2003). See especially the lengthy introduction by Peter Augustine Lawler.

regime is the greatest political achievement since Rome; but it is not the city laid up in heaven. Like every achievement within the *saeculum*, its justice is limited and mortal. The sun too will set on the era of American exceptionalism. When it does, those who have placed their fondest hopes in the promises of ideological politics may feel themselves dispossessed and demoralized; but those who have hearkened to the teachings of the traditionalists may find themselves, at last, at home.

CHAPTER TWO

Social Conservatism and the New Fusionism

Joseph Bottum

THERE IS NO CONSERVATISM in the United States and never has been—at least, if by "conservatism" we mean what we ought to mean: the preservation of the ancien régime, a government of throne and altar, and a perpetual endowment of medieval privileges for certain families, guilds, and classes. A nation born in political revolution may not appeal to the traditions of the polis as it existed before the revolution. And like a logical argument against the force of logic—or a grammatical complaint about the oppressive structure of grammar—a conservative rebellion against rebellion would only manage to instance, again, the thing it claims to undo. If we are conserving anything in America, it is the Revolution of 1776 and the founding generation's great experiment in freedom: an essentially anticonservative moment in human history.

This fact has consistently skewed the thought of everyone labeled, for one reason or another, a conservative. With *The Scarlet Letter*, we have American literature's most influential attack on the Mayflower Compact and the oppressive manners of close-knit communities—and it came from Nathaniel Hawthorne, cast by the majority of critics as the most conservative of New England's high nineteenth-century intellectuals. John C. Calhoun's thought may have informed the constitution of the Confederacy, but his speeches and letters—indeed, even his mostly abstract works of political theory, such as the posthumous *Disquisition on Government* and *Discourse on the Constitution and Government of the United States*—show that Calhoun was, in fact, a progressive social Darwinist *avant la lettre*, who believed in eugenic racism and the modern advance of positivistic science.

Perhaps conservatives among America's Catholics suffered less internal contradiction during the course of the nation's history by living in a democracy with the reservation that they would establish a Catholic monarchy if they could. "When I was young," F. Scott Fitzgerald once explained, "the boys in my street still thought that Catholics drilled in the cellar every night with the idea of making Pius the Ninth autocrat of this republic." But regardless of what the surrounding Protestant culture shiveringly imagined about Catholicism, did any American Catholics actually feel this way? From the nineteenth-century Orestes Brownson to the twentieth-century Michael Novak, Catholic political writers—conservative and liberal alike—seem to have spent most of their time explaining to their fellow Catholics how Catholicism doesn't actually contradict the American founding. This seems to suggest that not even Catholicism is a genuinely conservative force in American history—again, that is, if "conservatism" means a desire for the return of the ancien régime. As it happens, I believe that those American Catholic thinkers who argue the essential compatibility of the American Experiment and Catholicism are correct: Catholicism is not, in fact, the sole surviving medieval opponent of liberal democracy in the world—as Pope John Paul II's 1991 two-cheers-for-capitalism encyclical *Centessimus Annus* manifestly demonstrated.

But can that really be right? How can traditional Christianity not be an inherently conservative force in the modern world? Certainly, in some contemporary battles—the death penalty, for instance—Catholics can take what is now typically labeled a liberal position in

American politics. But beginning with the social issues tangled around abortion, serious Catholics are clearly attempting to conserve *some* principle that the radical modern impulse is determined to eliminate. This looks like a contradiction—an incoherence that, say, a typical sociological explanation would resolve by looking for the differences between the things Americans say they believe and the way they behave. But there is another possibility, which might save the intellectual integrity of American Catholic thought—the possibility that there is, in fact, a conservative element to the American proposition and that the insistence on the essential anticonservatism of American history must be mistaken.

The Catholics serve here merely as a particularly visible example. We could perform the same analysis with any of a dozen other groups, typically religious but not necessarily so. Like the Catholics, so the Evangelicals; and so the Southern agrarians; and so the neoconservatives; and so certain libertarians, for that matter. For each, a group that thinks itself American finds at some point that it is at odds not merely with this or that particular policy but also with the whole drift of things—the whole modern impulse that radicals insist is definingly American. And if the thinkers in these groups have not somehow ceased to be American, then the American founding—from the Declaration to the Constitution—has to be open to a dramatically different reading.

In book after book, particularly his influential 1953 volume, *The Conservative Mind*, Russell Kirk made a career out of eliminating as much revolution from the American Revolution as he possibly could. As it happens, he was correct that the founding involved much more than the high-liberal consensus of the mid-twentieth century usually allowed: Contrary to the mainstream views of, say, the majority of law-school professors in 1965, the Constitution wasn't simply a canal to get from the ocean of John Locke to the sea of John Stuart Mill. Rather, the founding drew upon deep waters of ancient Greek and

Roman thought, Protestant theology, French skepticism, Scottish commonsense philosophy, and British legal constitutionalism.

Of course, Kirk was also profoundly wrong in imagining that the American Revolution wasn't, nonetheless, a revolution charting a "new and more noble course." But there may be a way to rescue the Kirkian impulse by putting the emphasis in that phrase on the "more noble" rather than on the "new." The Founders were fond of asserting that they were building a "new order for the ages," but they were equally fond of asserting that they were rediscovering the ancient verities of human nature.

The distinction might be put this way: Was the American Revolution a setting free of the True Man or an experiment in creating the New Man? Did the Founders imagine that they were sweeping away the false accretions of prejudice to allow the reemergence of ancient principles, or did they believe they were establishing rights never before seen? Every utopia, W. H. Auden once remarked, is either backward-looking or forward-looking. The Americans gathered in Philadelphia in 1776 were hardly utopians in the sense that the French radicals and Marxist revolutionaries would later be. But it's still a meaningful question to ask whether the Founders generally had their eye back on the Old Eden or forward on the New Jerusalem.

The question seems answerable. There is a place to which the United States is entitled by "the Laws of Nature and of Nature's God," the Declaration of Independence maintains, and the nation's citizens "are endowed by their Creator with certain unalienable Rights." Surely this suggests an Edenist element in the American experiment. For his existence, the True Man requires a general recognition that there is such a thing as truth and, for that matter, such a thing as man. And if the founding concerned a perduring human nature and a natural law by which we aim at happiness, then there is something essential to conserve in American politics—thus, there are genuinely American conservatives. And, yet, this seems inadequate as an analysis of the American founding. Some such Kirkian move is mandatory if contemporary political conservatives are to justify their existence at all, and innumerable think tanks and institutions have made a huge investment in seeking the Revolution's conservative roots.

In some sense, the results have been gratifying, overturning seventy-five years of deliberate attempts—by progressive, then liberal, then radical historians and legal scholars—to teach the founding as an eighteenth-century secular-Enlightenment arrow aimed at the twentieth-century target of compulsory egalitarianism and radical liberty. Once again, religion affords the clearest example. In 2003, James Hutson put together an exhibition at the Library of Congress, illustrating the pervasive churchgoing and theological understanding of the signers of the Declaration of Independence and the Constitution. That same year Michael Novak published *On Two Wings*, collecting so many comments about God and church from the Founders that they seemed more theological obsessives than political theorists.

But apart from infuriating the likes of, say, Arthur Schlesinger Jr., how much does all this actually prove? The radical Enlightenment element of the American founding, the *revolution* of the Revolution, remains untouched, however nuanced our understanding of it may have to be. Perhaps we have overemphasized the written documents, ignoring the context—particularly the Protestant religious setting from the Mayflower Compact through the Great Awakening—in which they were written. Eighteenth-century America possessed a set of received ideas the Founders both relied upon and had to make concessions to. If the Constitution strikes a balance, then the conservative impulse requires insisting that the secular Enlightenment elements were counterweighted by other things—some of which may not be clearly in the Constitution at all.

Natural law, in all its complexity, as passed from the Jesuit Francisco Suarez to the Dutch and English Protestant scholastics, is perhaps the most obvious example, but there are innumerable others. Conservatives in America are those who begin to think, at some particular moment in the nation's history, that the butcher's thumb is coming down too hard on the radical side, and it has always made them nervous and peculiar.

We might call this the perpetual dilemma of American conservatism. Politically speaking, modernity *is* liberalism, and liberalism *is* modernity. Setting aside science, the political implications of which have not been fully explored by theorists, the turn to modern times is best defined by the rejection of the medieval structure of special privileges—by political liberalism, in other words. The most recent popular thinker to point this out in a persuasive way was Francis Fukuyama in *The End of History and the Last Man*. History didn't come to an end in 1989, he insisted; the fall of Soviet communism was merely the final proof of liberalism's implacable triumph. History, as the clash of genuine alternatives, actually ended right where G. W. F. Hegel said it did—in 1806, when Napoleon's victory at the Battle of Jena ensured that there no longer existed any real political possibilities other than liberalism.

But as modernity chugged bloodily along, while liberalism's triumph worked itself out over the next two hundred years, certain people felt the desire to get off the train. The twentieth century affords many examples. For some people, the impetus was the disaster of Socialist economics. For others, it was an inability to stomach abortion. For others, it was crime rates. For others, it was euthanasia. For a few recent converts, it is the threat of eugenic biotechnology. But for all of them, they reached a point where they decided "This is where I say, 'Enough.' This is a good place to stop."

Thus, Evangelicals wish to hold their position in the 1910s, the economic libertarians in the 1920s, the Southern agrarians in the 1940s, and the old *National Review* conservatives in the 1950s. Even after the great rush of Vatican II *aggiornamento*, Catholics essentially froze the modernity they were willing to accept at 1964. A variety of factors, most prominently the cultural upheavals of the 1960s, drew off the neoconservatives around 1972. Reagan's great conservative coalition of the 1980s, which was essentially a uniting of all these dissenters from the progressive liberal project under one big Republican tent, was enormously successful in closing off certain economic lines of development that advanced thought had once assumed were identical with modern liberalism.

But in other ways, particularly for social conservatives, the Reagan revolution was unsuccessful—as the rise of out-of-wedlock births, the apparent ineradicability of abortion, and our lockstep march toward biotechnology's Brave New World all demonstrate. And that is because there really never was much chance of success. Examined closely, each detraining group was seeking not to undo modernity but to freeze it at a particular moment—a moment when certain vestigial elements left over from the premodern world kept at bay the worst effects of modern times.

The problem is this: Lacking a coherent unmodern philosophy, we can offer no compelling reasons for modernity to stop where we wish it to. The economic and political battles against communism, by returning liberalism to its original course, certainly changed the direction of modernity, but they did nothing to slow modernity down. Take, once again, the question of religion. Over the past few decades, political scientists, sociologists, and scholars of the American founding have all pointed out that at least a smidgen of religious belief seems necessary to prevent modern liberalism from devouring its own political and economic gains. But this insight hasn't brought us much— a culture's religious belief doesn't derive from the desire, however sincere and well-informed, for that culture to have a religious belief. Meanwhile, since its Enlightenment beginning, modernity has conceived of religion as its great enemy, and the antireligious impulse of the modern world is still steaming on and on—unchecked by the conservative belief that this impulse ought to have stopped somewhere before this.

Consider, for another example, whether we could have had a liberalism against abortion. We did manage to find an anti-Communist liberalism, after all—however much the Communists insisted they were merely liberals in a hurry. Similarly, hard as it is to remember, there was a moment in the late 1960s when several liberal writers insisted that care for the poor and the weak demanded the rejection of abortion: The pro-abortion flag, wrote the then-Leftist Richard John Neuhaus in 1969, is "planted on the wrong side of the liberal-conservative divide"; it ought to be heartless Republicans who demand abortion and tender Democrats who wish the community of care to include the unborn. But the liberationist impulse was simply too strong and the sexual revolution too much fun. And so abortion came, despite those who wanted a modernity without it. They had bought a ticket this far; what means—what right, for that matter—did they have to stop the train from going further?

And now, modernity has brought us the biotech revolution, and yet other neoconservatives have reached the point of saying, "Enough. We must get off." But the question is how we are to stop now—for the steam engine of modernity is what drove us here, and everyone who finds eugenic biotechnology the step they cannot take has already accepted vast plains of modern development. There was a revealing moment, during testimony on the House of Representatives' bill to ban human cloning, when Congressman Ted Strickland of Ohio complained, "We should not allow theology, philosophy, or politics to interfere with the decision we make" on what ought to be a purely scientific matter. Like so much that was said in the cloning debate, this comment was both profoundly silly and profoundly true. Strickland was merely vulgar enough to say out loud what we all perfectly well understand: science has its own imperative force, and we cannot resist it without ceasing to be modern. You and I may get off the train, but the train is going on.

One of the least edifying spectacles in American conservatism is the determination, among those who've gotten off at later stations, to disparage those who got off at earlier stations. For the past seventy-five years, the soft Left in America has had a guilty conscience about its softness: the radicals always made the moderates feel a little bad. On the Right, too, there have been guilty consciences; but, curiously, these also have to do with Leftness. Although the Right, of course, trains its most intense fire at the Left, nearly everyone on the Right deems it necessary to find a more Rightist group *against* which to distinguish themselves. If "No enemies on the Left" is more or less the motto of liberals in America, "Always also enemies to the Right" seems to be a motto of conservatives.

A few figures have tried to hold together the ragtag collection of refugees: Ronald Reagan in his big-tent Republican party, Frank Meyer with his "fusionism" of libertarian and traditionalist writers in the *National Review* of the 1950s and 1960s, and Robert Bartley on the *Wall Street Journal* op-ed pages of the 1980s and 1990s. But mostly, when American writers and politicians have what seems a conservative impulse, they immediately distinguish themselves from the bulk of conservatism. There was a period in the 1980s in which nearly every article in the ostensibly liberal *New Republic* opened with something like: "I'm not one of those horrible conservatives, and I'd never vote for a Republican, but, gosh, there actually seems to be some merit to the idea of welfare reform"—or a strengthened military, or a mistrust of the United Nations, or any of a dozen other conservative topics.

Thus, the neoconservatives explain what is despicable about libertarians, and libertarians denounce the social conservatives—and on and on. Some of this disagreement is clearly necessary. The anti-Semitic neoconfederacy of the crowd gathered around *Chronicles* magazine deserves dismissal; as his eugenic embrace of evolutionary biology proves, its editor is not a seeker of the True Man but rather of a Calhoun-style New Man. So, too, the differences between the followers of Pat Buchanan and the writers for the *Weekly Standard*—

particularly about America's role in the world—cut to the heart of American policy and have genuine consequences. But the tone of conservative self-analysis is somehow off. Always missing is any reverent interpretation, meaning the ameliorative effort to find common ground or take opponents in the best sense. In a widely noticed 2003 article in *National Review*, David Frum declared that traditionalist conservatives "have turned their backs on their country. Now we turn our backs on them." In a more recent article in the *Public Interest*, Adam Wolfson took much the same line, more gently, in defending the neoconservatives. Meanwhile, Pat Buchanan and others on the Far Right fulminate in issue after issue of the *American Conservative*.

To say the *Weekly Standard* takes hard positions would be, in the contemporary political debate, an understatement. But the magazine, in general, tried to avoid publishing articles on conservative deviationism—thanks to the editorship of William Kristol, aided by the fact that the executive editor, Fred Barnes, is universally liked on the Right (and, to a lesser degree, by my own desire to run a strong back-of-the-book that isn't dominated by some conservative form of literary Stalinism). Still, even the *Weekly Standard* hasn't managed to avoid the temptation to find enemies on the Right. Despite my own editorial impulse toward a united front—a belief in the familial unity of the Right, born of my training among the Catholic neoconservatives—I cannot see how to put the cracked egg of conservatism back together. There seems no place in America these days for Frank Meyer's fusionism, or even Ronald Reagan's big-tent Republicanism, and it gives the Left an electoral advantage it doesn't otherwise deserve.

To find the missing piece, we would have to go back to the Founders and remember what it is that conservatism is supposed to be conserving—the element, the absence of which makes each conservative, however unconsciously, step off the liberal train. The answer, I'm afraid, will not please many libertarians, and some secularized neoconservatives and even a handful of the ultra-Rightists will not smile. For it is biblical religion, and the moral things held in place by Christianity, that the Constitution took for granted as the counterweight to Enlightenment radicalism.

There's a curious moment in the *Confessions* in which St. Augustine wrote that he could find many religious truths in the books of the philosophers. He could find that in the beginning was the Word. He could find that the Word was with God, and that the Word was God, and even that by the Word were all things made. But one truth he could not find in the philosophers was that the Word became flesh and dwelt among us. This may not seem a great difference: if we admit the metaphysical necessity of the Divine at the highest level of human philosophical thought, then it seems not much more to allow that God might occasionally concern Himself with human affairs. But, Augustine concluded, Christ is the truth that turns everything upside down; if God acts directly and willfully in human affairs, then He has broken history over His knee—choosing the foolish things of the world to confound the wise and the weak things to confound the mighty. And where in this is there any room to speak of the preeminence of politics or even the authority of justice?

St. Augustine was, relative to other Christian thinkers, a political realist, as *The City of God* demonstrates. But political philosophy, however theological or deistic it may be, cannot entirely accommodate this central fact of Christian revelation—this willingness to disdain political order and be true, though the heavens may fall as a result. And, yet, if the political order doesn't allow it, then the political benefits of religion cannot be held and democracy itself decays. "Whatever may be conceded to the influence of refined education on minds of peculiar structure," George Washington warned in his Farewell Address, "reason and experience both forbid us to expect that national morality can prevail in exclusion of religious principle." Public order in a constitutional democracy—the structure of liberalism that needs a people of virtue to maintain itself—seems to require the majority of citizens to believe in God. But no one, especially Americans, ever believed in God for the sake of public order in a constitutional democracy.

Liberalism, in other words, needs religion, and needs it in a variety of ways, from the simple genealogy of modernity's birth out of the spirit of Christendom to the complex reliance of modern times on a perduring set of premodern beliefs about right and wrong and good character. To reap the benefits it needs, a liberal democracy must allow religion to remain a possible authority—for individual conscience and for guiding legislative power—outside a modern state that longs to have no authority beyond the will of the people and the state's interpretation of individual rights. The United States as it naturally wants to be—what we might call the platonic ideal of America—contains a tension we must be careful not to resolve. What's more, it is a tension that the Founders themselves did not resolve and, I believe, were consciously careful not to resolve.

Whether the participants willed it or not, the American Revolution occurred in a Christian moment, giving the Founders certain advantages. From the political thought of St. Augustine to the Christian realism of Reinhold Niebuhr, innumerable arguments have suggested that biblical religion offers enormous public benefits. Indeed, Charles Murray argued—with his curious statistical reading of human greatness in *Human Accomplishment: The Pursuit of Excellence in the Arts and Sciences, 800 BC to 1950* (2004)—that Christendom's benefits are, by history's measure over the past thousand years, easily the greatest of any religion.

But the overwhelming Christian faith of America also presented the Founders with disadvantages, for the Bible cannot be entirely tamed to any public purpose or ethical reading. The tense and awkward solution of the Constitution derives, I think, from an awareness that the benefits and the dangers have the same root. To be a conservative is to recognize that if we lose either our extra-public religion or our Enlightenment use of public religion—if we break the delicately poised balance between the force of Christianity and the drive of modernity, if either side in this tension ever entirely vanquishes the other—the United States will cease to reflect its platonic ideal.

Of course, as support for the Wilsonian project of exporting liberty around the world, this isn't a particularly useful way of understanding democracy. Certain geographical analyses of the West's domination of the world since the Middle Ages—Jared Diamond's 1999 *Guns, Germs, and Steel,* for instance—seem to suggest the only hope for the poverty-stricken people in the Third World is to hire tugboats and have their countries dragged up to the Tropic of Cancer. In the same way, it has to be a little disheartening to tell, say, the Congolese that all they need for stable liberal democratic government is to begin as a colony of religious exiles, then read Locke and Montesquieu to pieces, then undergo a Great Awakening of Christian fervor—and then, at exactly the right moment, have a revolution, argue deeply about Federalism, and write a constitution. One feels there must be more to the success of the American Experiment than the fact that it occurred in a lucky moment during the Enlightenment struggles of faith and reason.

But quite what that "more" is seems hard to say. If I have correctly analyzed the real conservatism of the founding, then the most pressing conservative issue today ought to be the active participation of the culture in the most un-Christian act available at the moment—the thing most at odds with the background assumed by the Constitution. That is, of course, abortion. Whatever fusionism I fondly wish for the Right in American politics, my own ameliorative impulses will never extend to baby-killers or those who license infanticide. But, in fact, the murderousness of abortion is the single most defining political element today. It all comes down to abortion: every issue in contemporary politics is poisoned by abortion and reflects the cultural divide about its legality.

The pressures of the presidential campaign have helped translate the war in Iraq from what was primarily a foreign-policy issue to what is now overwhelmingly a culture-wars issue. A handful of foreign-policy neoconservatives may sympathize with legalized abortion, and a few traditionalists may mate their anti-abortion stands with distaste for the war. Once the translation is complete, however, the divisions about the war among ordinary voters match, to a startling degree, the divisions over abortion.

The British philosopher G. E. M. Anscombe, in a brilliant essay in 1958, pointed out that somewhere between John Stuart Mill in the nineteenth century and G. E. Moore in the twentieth, the British utilitarian tradition lost the ability to assert that the taking of innocent life is wrong. Anscombe also predicted that there would eventually come along someone willing to say that we should kill babies because utilitarianism offers no explanation of why we shouldn't. Anscombe intended this as the final rejection of utilitarian ethics—for, after all, killing babies is wrong, and a moral theory that arrives at the contrary conclusion must be mistaken.

But with Princeton University's Peter Singer, among others, we finally have utilitarians who have abandoned the last vestiges of cultural Christianity that skewed the purely philosophical structure of their ethics. They have accepted Anscombe's dilemma by denying that the taking of innocent life is always wrong. "John Paul II proclaims that the widespread acceptance of abortion is a mortal threat to the traditional moral order," Singer wrote in "Killing Babies Isn't Always Wrong," a 1995 article in the *London Spectator*. "I sometimes think that he and I at least share the virtue of seeing clearly what is at stake." For a believer, all of this demonstrates that there is nothing in the liberal philosophical tradition that can be counted upon to preserve, unaided by faith, the sanctity of innocent life.

With his 2002 book *Our Posthuman Future*, Francis Fukuyama went looking for a way, entirely within liberal philosophy, to argue against the motors of business and scientific inventiveness that are driving biotechnology; the work of Leon Kass at the President's Council on Bioethics has been directed toward much the same end. But Fukuyama and Kass have been, for the most part, defeated. The engine of eugenic biotechnology has chugged along undeterred, and the allies on the philosophical Left that the President's Council on Bioethics hoped to mobilize have proved mainly critics, despite their antibusiness impulses.

The reason for their defeat, of course, is abortion. Cloning, experimentation with the embryo, the whole panoply of biotechnological innovation, are wrapped up in the determination of the Left to ring yet another layer of prenatal murder around the right to abortion— the Left's unwillingness to admit the least theoretical crack in the pro-abortion wall. For much the same reason, the literary Left in America, which proudly claims to own the heritage of English literature, has embraced the biotechnological revolution, despite the fact that the literary imagination—from Mary Shelley's *Frankenstein* to Aldous Huxley's *Brave New World*—has never pictured the prospect of manufactured human beings with much joy. Nor, for that matter, has the literary imagination, from Robert Louis Stevenson's *Dr. Jekyll and Mr. Hyde* to H. G. Wells's *The Island of Dr. Moreau*, been much taken with scientists who manipulate the deep things of life just because they can.

There are a range of other social conservative issues at the moment, beginning with same-sex marriage and extending through education reform, but to a large degree, the divisions on these issues track the divisions on abortion. With only minor exceptions, the people who feel strongly on one side of the abortion debate are the people who feel strongly on one side of the same-sex marriage debate. Some of the contemporary issues involve narrower questions of church-state relations. Last year, the Ninth Circuit did what it could to help President Bush's re-election campaign by declaring the phrase "under God" an unconstitutional addition to the Pledge of Allegiance. Again, however, the issues involve the role of religion in America, and they cycle back to the abortion question.

Where opposition to communism once held the Right together—

it was critical to Meyer's fusionism and Reagan's Republicanism—little unites conservatives today or forces them to play nice with one another. But there may be more linking the Right than appears on the surface. The neoconservatives gathered around the *Weekly Standard* might appear to have made a fairly cynical bargain with social conservatives, from the Evangelicals Chuck Colson and Gary Bauer to the Catholics George Weigel and Richard John Neuhaus: "If you support us in an activist and moralist foreign policy, we'll support you in the pro-life fight—with all the social implications that follow." And, yet, the actual creation of this fusion resulted from mutual persuasion not political bargaining. Indeed, the prior opposition to abortion by the Catholic, Evangelical, and Jewish neoconservatives—and the mutual trust that opposition inspired—is one of the things that drove the social conservatives to support, in general, the invasion of Iraq.

In 1995, Jerry Z. Muller published a cover story in the *New Republic* entitled "The Conservative Case for Abortion." His utilitarian argument that "the right-to-life position undermines [the] fundamentally conservative effort to strengthen families" didn't persuade many on the Right: It may be true, as Muller wrote, that "conservatives have long assumed that government should promote those social norms that encourage the creation of decent men and women," but conservatives have long assumed as well that decent men and women don't slaughter their young. If anything seemed designed to persuade social conservatives that philosophical analysis could not be counted upon to defend the innocent, this was it.

Yet, Muller was right in another way. After the fall of Eastern European communism in 1989, there was a narrow window in which it still seemed possible to disunite the old *Commentary* and *Public Interest*–style neoconservatives and the new Evangelical and Catholic social conservatives. There were natural tensions between them, as instanced when the journal *First Things* started a firestorm by running a symposium on judicial tyranny called "The End of Democracy?"

CHAPTER THREE

The Moral
Foundations of
Modern Libertarianism

Randy E. Barnett

ALTHOUGH THE CLASSICAL liberal political philosophy that empha-
sizes individual liberty is centuries old, the modern American variant,
known as "libertarianism," can be traced to the early 1960s. The story
has been told before,[1] but I trace the modern libertarian intellectual
movement to the split between Ayn Rand and Murray Rothbard.
Rand had popularized the centrality of liberty as defined by property
rights and as grounded in an Aristotelian version of natural law. Rothbard, an economist, further developed these elements while emphasizing the role of Austrian economics in explaining how liberty and
the free market operate. Significantly, Rothbard also adopted an anar-
chist stance toward monopolistic government. Although none of the
component parts of Rothbardianism were entirely original, it is fair
to say that his distinctive combination of Austrian economics, Aristotelian natural law ethics, Lockean natural rights, noninterventionist
foreign policy, and individualist anarchism made up a distinctive

1. See Jerome Tuccille, *It Usually Begins with Ayn Rand* (New York: Stein &
Day, 1971).

package that captured the imagination of a cadre of young intellectuals in the 1960s and 1970s, who went on to become influential in their own right in the 1980s and 1990s.

Rothbard shared another and less attractive quality of Rand's that would prove historically significant: his insistence on complete ideological purity. Most who entered his orbit in the 1970s were independent thinkers; otherwise, they would not have escaped the dominant statist orthodoxy of their schooling. Yet their very independence eventually put them at odds with Rothbardian orthodoxy. Almost every intellectual who entered his orbit was eventually spun off, or self-emancipated, for some deviation or another. For this reason, the circle around Rothbard was always small, and what should have been his intellectual legacy was stunted and obscured.

In a similar vein, Rothbard was also jealous of any competition for the hearts and minds of libertarians. In this regard, the principal objects of his ire, and that of some in his intellectual circle, were Milton Friedman and Friedrich Hayek. Friedman not only held a prestigious academic appointment at the University of Chicago, in contrast with Rothbard's position at Brooklyn Polytechnic, but he also achieved national prominence with his regular column in *Newsweek* magazine. Rothbardians strongly criticized the "utilitarianism" of Friedman's defense of liberty and his willingness to offer government programs, such as school vouchers and the negative income tax, that compromised with, rather than opposed outright, statism. Friedman's embrace of "neoclassical" economics, rather than Austrianism, was another object of severe criticism.

As a pioneer of Austrian economics, Hayek was obviously on stronger methodological grounds than Friedman, though Hayek rejected the strict praxiological methodology of his and Rothbard's teacher, Ludwig von Mises, whose approach stressed the role of deduction from axiomatic first principles of economics.[2] If anything,

---

2. See Ludwig von Mises, *Human Action: A Treatise on Economics* (New Haven,

Hayek was, for most of his career, much less ideologically libertarian in his policy proscriptions than even Friedman. And Hayek never warmed to the concept of natural rights, which he associated with "French" rationalism. Given Rothbard's professional insecurity, Hayek's positions at the London School of Economics and then at the Committee on Social Thought at the University of Chicago were not a plus. Mises himself, of course, was neither a natural rights adherent nor a radical libertarian, but he did labor in obscurity as an academic—obtaining only a business school appointment—a disgraceful treatment with which his protégé Rothbard could strongly identify.

I relate this story with no desire to deprecate the memory of Murray Rothbard. Few thinkers had as much influence on my intellectual development as did he. Beginning with his writings when I was in college, especially *For a New Liberty*,[3] and continuing with our personal association throughout law school, I came to internalize the Rothbardian paradigm and, to a large extent, still work within it.[4] In one way or another, most current intellectual leaders of the modern libertarian movement originated in the Rothbardian camp. But the story is worth retelling because it helps explain a feature of modern libertarianism that has been on the wane for some time as Rothbard's influence declined during his lifetime and after his death: the radical disjuncture between rights and consequences. In the Rothbardian approach, rights were to be defended on purely "moral" grounds—employing a Randian form of Aristotelianism.[5] The idea that adher-

---

CT: Yale University Press, 1949). For Rothbard's expansion of this methodology, see Murray N. Rothbard, *Man, Economy, and State: A Treatise on Economic Principles* (2 volumes). (Princeton, NJ: D. Van Nostrand, 1962).

3. See Murry N. Rothbard, *For a New Liberty: The Libertarian Manifesto* (New York: Macmillan, 1973). A revised edition was published in paperback by Colliers in 1978.

4. I discuss the development of my interest in libertarianism at somewhat greater length in Randy E. Barnett, *The Structure of Liberty: Justice and the Rule of Law* (Oxford: Clarendon Press, 1978), vii–x.

5. See Murray N. Rothbard, *The Ethics of Liberty* (Atlantic Highlands, NJ: Humanities Press, 1982).

ence to properly defined moral rights yielded superior social consequences was treated like a happy coincidence, though one that was quickly emphasized in nearly every discussion of libertarian public policy. Any "utilitarian" thinker, such as Friedman or Hayek, no matter how libertarian his conclusions, was to be treated with skepticism. Friedman and Hayek's own policy compromises with statism evidenced how utilitarians were not to be trusted as true libertarians.

Even before his death in 1995, however, Rothbard's insistence on complete agreement from his admirers, and his willingness to shuck any deviationists, undermined the radical disjunction between his approach and that of consequentialists. One by one, as his most brilliant adherents left the fold, they rediscovered the relationship between rights and consequences long known to classical natural rights thinkers, who predated the modern philosophical divide between Kantian moralists on the one hand and Benthamite utilitarians on the other. Before long, former Rothbardians incorporated into their methods the insights of Hayek and developed an appreciation for the libertarian commitment of Friedman as well, though admittedly both men became much more radically libertarian as they aged and, therefore, easier for radical libertarians to embrace.

Perhaps the person most responsible for moving to a new synthesis of Rothbardian radical libertarianism with consequentialism was a former fair-haired Rothbardian named George H. Smith. Although Smith authored few works in political theory—his most influential publications concerned atheism, another aspect of Rothbardian thought about which agreement was *not* demanded[6]—in a few essays and many lectures and other oral presentations, he reconnected modern libertarianism with its classical liberal roots. After immersing himself in the writings of classical natural rights theorists, Smith developed, and conveyed to others in his lectures, a renewed appre-

6. George H. Smith, *Atheism: The Case Against God* (Buffalo, NY: Prometheus Books, 1980).

ciation for the classical liberal reconciliation of moral rights with that of consequentialism.

Whether due to Smith's influence, libertarians no longer argue, as they once did in the 1970s, about whether libertarianism must be grounded on moral rights or on consequences. Libertarians no longer act as though they must choose between these two moral views; in this chapter, I explain why they need not.

Transcending Rights and Consequences

Libertarians need not choose between moral rights and consequences because theirs is a *political*, not a moral, philosophy—one that can be shown to be compatible with various moral theories, which, as we shall see, is one source of libertarianism's appeal. Moral theories based on either moral rights or on consequentialism purport to be "comprehensive," insofar as they apply to all moral questions to the exclusion of all other moral theories. Although the acceptance of one of these moral theories entails the rejection of all others, libertarian moral rights philosophers such as Eric Mack, Loren Lomasky, Tibor Machan, Douglas Rasmussen, and Douglas Den Uyl on the one hand, and utilitarians such as David Friedman on the other, can embrace libertarian political theory with equal fervor. How can this be?

As George Smith rediscovered, before Bentham and Kant, classical natural rights "liberals" employed a mixture of moral rights and consequentialist arguments in defense of the political protection of certain natural rights. Within modern libertarian political theory, moral rights and consequentialism can each be viewed as a method of analyzing how humans ought to behave. Because the use of any method of analysis, including the application of moral theories, is fallible, political theorists should be sensitive both to where moral rights and consequentualist analysis reach the same results and to where they differ.

First, if both methods tend to reach the same results in entirely different ways, then each method can provide an analytic check on the other. Because any of our analytic methods may err or be used to deceive, we can use one method to confirm the results that appear to be supported by the other. Analogously, after adding a column of figures from top to bottom, we sometimes double-check the sum by adding the figures again from bottom to top or by using a calculator. Just as we rely upon institutional rivalries between branches of government to protect against error and deception, we may also rely upon "conceptual rivalries" between different methods of normative inquiry. One way that moral rights and consequentialist modes of analysis may be functionally compatible within a political theory, therefore, is by providing a conceptual "checks and balances" mechanism by which errors in our normative analysis may be detected and prevented.

Second, only if we rely upon multiple modes of analysis can we assess the degree of confidence that we should have in a conclusion recommended by any single mode of analysis. Because we know that no evaluative method is infallible, the more valid methods that point in the same direction, the more confident we may be that this is the direction in which to move. Conversely, a divergence of results between two valid methods suggests problems that may exist at the level of application of a method or deep inside the method itself. Divergent results from competing methodologies recommend not only that we proceed cautiously but also that we carefully reconsider our methods and their application so we can discover, if possible, the source of the divergence. A second way, then, that an analysis of both moral rights and consequences may be functionally compatible is that when we rely on competing modes of analysis, *convergence of results begets confidence* and *divergence of results stimulates discovery.*[7] This is

7. See Randy E. Barnett, "The Virtues of Redundancy in Legal Thought," *Cleveland-State Law Review* 38 (1990): 153–68.

especially true when multiple methods each capture some feature of the world that most everyone thinks is salient.

The Salience of Moral Rights and Consequentialist Analyses

A moral rights analysis, by which I mean rights derived either from teleological or deontological methods, is salient because it takes seriously the individual. Moral rights that are properly defined protect the highly valued "private" sphere. Put another way, moral rights analysis views the actions of individuals (and the associations to which they consensually belong) from the perspective of the individual. The specialized evaluative techniques this analysis employs are conducive to elaborating this individualist perspective. Because we all are individuals, the idea of moral rights has wide appeal. We have a natural interest in the protection of our rights, and our empathy causes us to be concerned about the protection of the rights of others.

In contrast, consequentialist analysis is salient because it takes seriously the wide-reaching and highly dispersed effects that the actions of individuals and their associations may often have on others. Consequentialist analysis can be seen as protecting a "public" sphere. Although consequentialist analysis is often couched in terms of how "society" views the consequences of individual actions, this anthropomorphic metaphor can be avoided by saying that consequentialist analysis views the actions of individuals from the perspective of the other persons with whom those individuals live in society. Because we are all affected by the actions of others, the consequentialist perspective also has wide appeal. We are concerned about the consequences to us of other persons' actions, and our empathy causes us also to be concerned about the consequences of such actions for others.

In other words, both moral rights and consequentialism are not only foundational moral theories, but they are also useful heuristics—

ways of thinking and solving problems, quickly, efficiently, and making the most of what we already know—within a political theory. Even so, at some point, both of these perspectives lose their salience. Moral rights analysis becomes unappealing when it advocates the protection of moral rights "though heavens may fall." Most people care about the domain of discretionary actions that rights protect, but they also care about the falling of the heavens. Consequentialist analysis becomes unappealing when it sacrifices the domain of action protected by moral rights in the interest of a completely impersonal standard of value—"utils," wealth maximization, and so on. Most people do not want to sacrifice their liberty to act, even if such sacrifices significantly benefit others.

The creative tension between moral rights and consequentalist analysis reflects a tension that is central to the classical liberal core of the modern libertarian project. On the one hand, in contrast with more elitist approaches, liberalism seeks to protect the dignity of the common person, meaning all persons qua human beings. On the other hand, liberalism has always acknowledged the need to prevent the actions of some from adversely affecting the interests of others. Nor has individualist-flavored liberalism ever denied the importance of the community in which individuals reside. Liberalism always sits betwixt and between these two great concerns, a position that has led some critics of liberalism to complain of its internal dialectic, inherent tensions, or fundamental contradictions.

It would be mistaken to conclude that this undeniable tension between individual and community, between self and others, is a contradiction in a logical sense. Aristotle, no stranger to logic (albeit Aristotelian), held that virtue consists in seeking the mean between two extremes. This does not represent a middle-of-the-road position but rather the quality of suitableness. In this sense, liberalism is like Aristotelian virtue ethics—it attempts to supply a conceptual and institutional structure that is exquisitely poised between the individual and others.

The types of political actions that pass muster from the points of view of both moral rights and consequences—or neither—are "easy cases" in which we can be quite confident in our judgment. The types of political actions about which moral rights and expediency provide conflicting assessments, however, are "hard cases" that call upon us to reconsider our analysis or to further refine our analytic techniques. Until such time as a conflict between modes of analysis is resolved, we must tread cautiously; and the fact that caution is required is itself worth knowing.

And, yet, the fact that we must act politically in the face of conflicting modes of analysis or heuristics suggests that the "compatibilist" picture I have painted to this point is incomplete. How is it that we are not frozen in our tracks until conflicts between moral rights and consequentialist perspectives are resolved? There is yet another mechanism of choice that functions alongside analyses of rights and consequences. This mechanism is not fully appreciated by many Libertarians, whether Rothbardians or utilitarians like Friedman; rather, it is revealed by a more Hayekian evolutionary approach.

The Missing Link: Legal Evolution and the Rule of Law

The rhetoric of philosophers and economists would lead one to think that a comprehensive analysis of moral rights or a comprehensive analysis of consequences would eventually discover the full panoply of norms upon which law should be based. But neither mode of analysis can accomplish such a feat. Instead, both rights theorists and consequentialists get their starting points from conventional practice. In the Anglo-American legal system, the conventions of practice have typically been generated by the spontaneously evolving process known as the common law. As Lon Fuller put it:

> It can be said that law is the oldest and richest of the social sciences.
> . . . Economists who have exhausted the resources of their own
> science turn to the law for insight into the nature of the institutional

arrangements essential for a free economy. Philosophers find in the
law a discipline lacking in their own sometimes errant studies—the
discipline, namely, that comes of accepting the responsibility for
rendering decisions by which men can shape their lives.[8]

That philosophical and economic analyses are typically used to
subject established conventional legal principles to critical scrutiny is
of methodological significance. It suggests that, even taken together,
moral rights and consequentialist analyses cannot explain the *discovery*
of legal norms that would satisfy their critical demands. It further
suggests that moral rights and consequentialist analyses are simply a
part of how legal norms are discovered. Something more is required.

Although this is not how philosophers and economists usually
view their own disciplines, moral rights and consequentialism can be
viewed as highly useful ways of evaluating the inherited, traditional,
or received wisdom. Judges must decide cases even in the absence of
an ironclad moral rights or consequentialist analysis. Indeed, for most
of our legal history, there was little such systematic rational analysis
available at all. Yet, somehow, common-law processes managed to
develop doctrines that pass muster by moral rights and consequentialist standards. What made this possible?

Unlike either modern philosophy or economics, legal decision
making is casuistic.[9] The need to resolve a multitude of real disputes
or cases, each with its own peculiar facts, is the engine that drives
legal evolution forward. This engine produces a body of reported
outcomes of countless cases in which contending parties have laid
claims of right both to some resource (including the resource that
would be used to satisfy a monetary damage award) and to the reasons
given by judges for these outcomes (as well as dissenting and con-

---

8. See Lon L. Fuller, *Anatomy of the Law* (New York: Praeger, 1968), 84–108
(presenting ten distinctive characteristics of the common-law process).

9. For a sympathetic explication of case-by-case, or "casuistic," reasoning, see
Albert R. Jonsen and Stephen Toulmin, *The Abuse of Casuistry* (Berkeley: University
of California Press, 1988).

curring judicial opinions). From this diverse body of case law emerge dominant conventions—sometimes called the "majority rule"—as well as other rival conventions that may be called the "minority rule."

Once discovered by legal institutions, these evolved conventional rules that govern claims of right may then be subjected to critical reason in the form of a mixture of moral rights and consequentialist analysis. Yet, for the traditional conventions produced by the adjudicative process to provide more than a random starting point for a critical analysis based on moral rights and consequences, it is not enough that cases simply be resolved. The *way* in which disputed claims of right are resolved determines whether the results reached by a legal system can evolve into promising conventional standards of right conduct, which can then be subjected to and, in the main, survive the normative scrutiny of critical reason based on moral rights and consequentialist analysis. Only if the processes that resolve disputes do so in certain ways can we take the views we receive from these processes as a form of wisdom. Similarly, the way that legislation is enacted either supports or undermines the likelihood that such legislation is substantively justified.

The form that enables dispute-resolution processes to produce "judgments" that are knowledgeable enough to withstand critical scrutiny on the basis of moral rights or consequences can be summarized under the rubric of "the rule of law." I discuss elsewhere, at some length, the procedural elements that help ensure decisions that will pass the scrutiny of rights and consequentialist analysis.[10] Lon Fuller provided the best summary of these formal constraints,[11] which he called the "internal morality of law" and understood to be

A procedural version of natural law, though to avoid misunder-

10. See Barnett, *The Structure of Liberty*, 84–131.
11. See Lon L. Fuller, *The Morality of Law*, rev. ed. (New Haven, CT: Yale University Press, 1969), 38–39 (listing eight formal characteristics of legality); Lon L. Fuller, "The Forms and Limits of Adjudication," 92 *Harvard Law Review* 93 (1978): 353 (discussing the formal requirements of adjudication).

standing the word "procedural" should be assigned a special and expanded sense so that it would include, for example, a substantive accord between official action and enacted law. The term "procedural" is, however, broadly appropriate as indicating that we are concerned, not with the substantive aims of legal rules, but with the ways in which a system of rules for governing human conduct must be constructed and administered if it is to be efficacious and at the same time remain what it purports to be.[12]

Decisions made according to the formal standards provided by the rule of law may produce an elaborate set of decisions, consisting both of results (the facts of the case plus who won) and of articulated rationales for the results. When a sufficiently elaborate set of decisions (results and rationales) has developed, it becomes possible to subject this set of practices to systematic rational appraisal, including the appraisal provided by what Fuller termed the "external morality of law."[13]

Some might respond that if both moral rights and consequentialist modes of analysis are useful ways of improving past practices that have evolved as part of a process governed by the rule of law, what then is the criterion or criteria by which we decide that something is or is not an "improvement"? Unless we know the standard by which improvement is to be measured, how can we say that either method improves current practices? Unless we know the ends of the legal system, how can we know they are being served? To answer the question of ends, goes this response, requires a choice between the normative standard of justice based on moral rights or the normative standard of utility based on the maximization of beneficial consequences. In making this choice, we cannot escape the essential incompatibility of rights and consequences as moral theories. Ultimately, one approach must either be subordinate to or subsume the other.

Although some idea of improvement is indeed needed to appre-

12. Fuller, *The Morality of Law*, 96–97.
13. Ibid., 96.

ciate the roles played by moral rights, consequentialist analysis, and the rule of law, this conception of improvement need not be based exclusively on any one of these three perspectives. Rather than comprehensive evaluative theories, all three approaches can be recast within a political theory as problem-solving devices. Viewed in this light, all of these modes of analysis are themselves means, not ends. To provide the requisite idea of improvement, one must identify not so much an ultimate standard of value but rather the ultimate *problem* that needs legal coercion to solve. We can then see how an evolutionary common-law decision-making process and modes of critical analysis, such as those provided by moral rights and consequentialist methods, all contribute to solving the relevant problem. Moreover, other processes and methods of rational analysis, such as rational bargaining analysis or game theory, may also be useful.

The Ends of Justice:
Providing the Conditions of Social Order

According to classical liberals, the fundamental problem facing every society may be summarized as follows: given that the actions of each person in society are likely to have effects on others, on what conditions is it possible for persons to live and pursue happiness in society with other persons? "Social order" is the term traditionally used to describe the state of affairs that permits every person to live and pursue happiness in society with others. F. A. Hayek offered the following definition of the general concept of "order":

> [A] state of affairs in which a multiplicity of elements of various kinds are so related to each other that we may learn from our acquaintance with some spacial or temporal part of the whole to form correct expectations concerning the rest, or at least expectations which have a good chance of proving correct.[14]

14. F. A. Hayek, *Law, Legislation and Liberty*, vol. 1 (Chicago: University of Chicago Press, 1973), 36.

Unfortunately, this term has come to be associated with ordering schemes imposed from above by totalitarian regimes. As Hayek noted, "[t]he term 'order' has, of course, a long history in the social sciences, . . . but in recent times it has generally been avoided, largely because of the ambiguity of its meaning and its frequent association with authoritarian views. We cannot do without it, however"[15] For this reason, perhaps the term "coordination" better captures the problem of achieving what Hayek called an "order of actions."[16] Whatever the terminology, some way must be found to permit persons to act so that their actions do not obstruct the actions of others.

This rendition of the fundamental problem of human society contains a number of classical liberal or libertarian presuppositions. I view libertarianism as a subset of classical liberalism, and on these following five points all or most classical liberals agree. First, libertarians recognize the existence and value of individual persons. Second, libertarians place value on the ability of all persons to live and pursue happiness. Third, libertarians use the phrase "pursuit of happiness" because they believe that only the protection of actions, rather than a guaranty of results, can potentially be afforded to everyone and that, in any event, no identifiable set of results would provide happiness for everyone. Fourth, libertarians recognize that people live in society with others and that the actions of one may have both positive and negative effects on others. Fifth, libertarians maintain that it is possible to find conditions, or ground rules, that would provide all, or nearly all, persons living in society the opportunity to pursue happiness without depriving others of the same opportunity.

Of course, although they are widely shared, each of these presuppositions is and has always been, controversial. For this reason, classical liberalism is, and has always been, controversial, just as libertarianism is today. Where controversy arises over any of these

15. Ibid., 35.
16. See ibid., 98–101 (discussing the role played by legal institutions in maintaining "an ongoing order of actions").

presuppositions, it must be thrashed out in the appropriate forum. Given these presuppositions, however, the next step is to ask how to solve the problem of achieving coordination. In the next section, I suggest how "natural rights" address this problem.

The Imperative of Certain Natural Rights

The term "natural rights" means many things to many people, and I shall not try to compare my conception with that of others. For present purposes, it is enough to identify two significant features of natural rights thinking. First, writers in the classical natural rights tradition attempted to address, in a realistic manner, the problem of social order. Sometimes they referred to this as the "common good," referring not to some public good that transcends the persons living in society with others but to those basic requirements that all such persons share. Second, they addressed this problem with a mixture of what we would today consider moral rights and consequentialist analyses, from which they concluded that laws and political systems should be assessed against certain principles that they described as natural rights.

Let me briefly summarize the liberal approach to natural rights that I have identified and defended at length elsewhere.[17] When living in society with others, humans need to act. Their actions require the use of physical resources, including their bodies; however, because of scarcity, their actions unavoidably affect others. Given that nearly all human action affects others in some way, how are actions to be regulated so that individuals may act in pursuit of their own happiness, without impeding the similar pursuit by others?

To answer this, a natural rights approach attempts to establish an appropriate time and place for the actions of different persons by examining certain features of the world that are common to all, at

17. See Barnett, *The Structure of Liberty.*

least under circumstances we would consider to be normal. Abstracting from normal circumstances gives rise to comparatively abstract principles that presumptively govern the use of resources, unless it can be shown that extraordinary circumstances exist to support the creation of an exception—itself defeasible—to the rule.[18] The contours of this scheme of defeasible principles and exceptions define, in general terms, the natural rights of all persons—rights that are not themselves individually defeasible.

The basic rights produced at this stage are quite abstract. For persons to live and pursue happiness in society with others, persons need to act at their own discretion. This is made possible by recognizing a sphere of jurisdiction over physical resources—including their own bodies—that provides them with discretionary control, or "liberty," over these resources. Put another way, persons need to be at liberty to act freely within the realm of their jurisdictions, and these jurisdictions have both temporal and spatial boundaries.

The term for this bounded jurisdiction is the "right of property,"[19] with property given its older meaning of "proprietorship." One was said to have property in an object or in one's body.[20] Property, in this sense, refers not to an object but to a right to control physical resources—a right that cannot normally be displaced without either the consent or wrongful conduct of the right-holder. Some of these property rights are alienable and others are inalienable. Persons need to be able to consensually transfer their alienable rights or jurisdiction to others. The term for this is the "right of freedom of contract."[21]

18. The historical practice of using presumptive precepts within different stages of analysis and the virtues of this technique are discussed in Richard A Epstein, "Pleading and Presumptions," *University of Chicago Law Review* 40 (1973): 556; see also George Fletcher, "The Right and the Reasonable," *Harvard Law Review* 98 (1985): 949 (distinguishing between "flat" and "structured" modes of legal analysis).

19. I, following Hayek, refer to this as "the right of several property."

20. See, for example, John Locke, "An Essay Concerning the True Origin, Extent and End of Civil Government," in *Two Treatises of Civil Government*, ch. V, § 27 (London 1690) ("every man has a property in his own person").

21. The "right of freedom of contract" has two dimensions: freedom *to* contract

In addition, persons need to bring previously unowned physical resources into a state of proprietorship (the "right of first possession"), use force to defend their rights (the "right of self-defense"), and receive compensation for any interferences with the use and enjoyment of the resources that they own (the "right of restitution"). In addition, some libertarians think there is also a natural "right to punish" rights violators.

Thus, these fundamental inalienable rights of classical liberalism that lie at the very core of libertarianism are the rights of Several Property, Freedom of Contract, First Possession, Self-Defense, and Restitution. In the abstract, all these rights are inalienable: persons always retain the right to perform the types of acts that these rights sanction. However, while the right to one's person is inalienable, particular physical items that are brought into a state of ownership may be alienated by consent, and even an inalienable right may be forfeited by wrongdoing.

Abstract natural rights are like a cheat sheet for a multiple-choice exam. Although they can often distinguish right action from wrong, they do not provide all the reasons that some actions should be thought right and others wrong; therefore, they are often unpersuasive unless bolstered by more explicitly consequentialist analysis. Nonetheless, such a cheat sheet can obviate the need for costly and potentially tragic "social experiments" that may be recommended by faulty consequentialist analyses.[22] Even when such experiments are destructive, there is often no efficient way to terminate them. Perhaps more than others, libertarians contend that it is far better to use an abstract natural rights analysis to look before one leaps. But if seriously adverse consequences were ever shown to result from adhering to the out-

---

(the right to transfer rights by consent) and freedom *from* contract (the right to be free from transfers without the right-holder's consent).

22. I make this methodological argument in the context of drug prohibition in Randy E. Barnett, "Bad Trip: Drug Prohibition and the Weakness of Public Policy," *Yale Law Journal* 103 (1994): 2593–629.

comes recommended by a natural rights analysis, that analysis would have to be reexamined and perhaps revised.

Lastly, to perform their function of enabling social order, natural rights—which are nothing more than concepts or constructs—must be implemented by effective institutions that are capable of protecting and enforcing these rights. Such institutions must themselves be subject to substantive and procedural "constitutional" constraints to ensure that the very institutions whose mission it is to protect rights do not end up violating them.[23]

The Right and the Good

Natural rights allow persons and associations the jurisdiction to decide how certain physical resources—including their own bodies—should be used. Such jurisdiction is bounded, and the boundaries must be enforced by institutions governed by the rule of law. These institutions, in turn, produce the cases and decisions that lead to important refinements of our understanding of the basic precepts of justice. Legal evolution requires a constant rotation among these modes of analysis—the rule of law and justice based on both moral rights and consequentialist analyses—as well as others. Viewed in static terms, this process may appear circular. Viewed as an evolutionary process, however, it more nearly resembles a propeller, the rotation of which enables a ship to move forward in the water.

Determining the content of the rights that define justice does not, however, exhaust the whole issue of how persons ought to behave. Although natural rights purport to be universal, based as they are in abstractions that apply in all places and at all times, these rights are not comprehensive. Identifying the bounded rights that people have to control physical resources does not specify how people should exercise their rights. For example, should one be an egoist exercising one's

23. See Randy E. Barnett, *Restoring the Lost Constitution: The Presumption of Liberty* (Princeton, NJ: Princeton University Press, 2004), ch. 1–3.

rights solely to benefit oneself, an altruist exercising one's rights solely to benefit others, or somewhere in between?

Classical natural rights theorists sometimes distinguished between "perfect" and "imperfect" rights and duties. Perfect rights referred to those rights that create an enforceable duty in others, as in "I have a perfect right to this land." Imperfect rights identify duties toward oneself and others that do not justify the use of coercion. The natural rights analysis described above addresses only the question of enforceability. The matter of unenforceable individual duties must be addressed by the broader inquiry known as natural law ethics.[24] Lon Fuller made a similar distinction between the "morality of aspiration" (what I am calling "the good," which is addressed by natural law ethics) and the "morality of duty" (what I am calling "justice," which is addressed by natural rights):

> The morality of aspiration . . . is the morality of the Good Life, of excellence, of the fullest realization of human powers. . . . Where the morality of aspiration starts at the top of human achievement, the morality of duty starts at the bottom. It lays down the basic rules without which an ordered society is impossible, or without which an ordered society directed toward certain specific goals must fail of its mark. . . . It does not condemn men for failing to embrace opportunities for the fullest realization of their powers. Instead, it condemns them for failing to respect the basic requirements of social living.[25]

Much needless controversy about natural rights is generated by the idea that an adequate rights theory must address not only the problem of unjust conduct that justifies legal enforcement but also the problem of good, virtuous, or ethical conduct. The general issue of good conduct far exceeds the domain of natural rights, with one significant exception: although a natural rights analysis seeks to permit

---

24. See Randy E. Barnett, "A Law Professor's Guide to Natural Law and Natural Right," *Harvard Journal of Law and Public Policy* 20 (1997): 655–81.
    25. Fuller, *The Morality of Law*, 5–6.

the pursuit of differing conceptions of the good life, it does prevent, at least indirectly, certain conceptions of the good from being achieved. In this sense, though a natural rights approach is universal with respect to just conduct but not comprehensive with respect to good conduct, it still excludes some conceptions of the good. It is particularly incompatible with any comprehensive theory of the good that requires overriding the requirements of justice defined by natural rights.

A natural rights approach solves the problem of social order by placing certain restrictions on the means one may use to pursue happiness. Consequently and unavoidably, those who believe that their pursuit of happiness requires them to use the very means that are proscribed cannot be permitted to do so. For example, those who find gratification in having unconsensual sexual intercourse with others may not pursue this course of action because it runs afoul of the principles of justice that make possible the pursuit of happiness of each person living in society with others. Of course, such conduct is not only unjust but also ethically despicable. That an action is ethically despicable, however, is neither necessary nor sufficient to justify its legal prohibition.

In addition to restricting "bad" conduct that is also unjust, a natural rights approach sometimes prohibits coercively mandating "good" conduct. Earlier I described the legal enterprise—with its rivalrous components of the rule of law and natural rights based on both a moral rights and a consequentialist analysis—as the means by which we solve the problem of social order. But social order is not the only problem facing persons living in society with others. What about the provision of food, water, shelter, and other material needs, not to mention spiritual needs, of life? Does not the legal enterprise also have an important role to play in the provision, or at least the distribution, of all these goods?

Although I address this question at greater length elsewhere,[26]

26. See Barnett, *The Structure of Liberty*, 303–28.

some basic methodological observations can be made here. First, one ought not use the mechanisms that enable social order to exist to address other pressing problems if doing so seriously undermines the ability of these mechanisms to continue to address the problem of social order. The attainment of social order is a prerequisite for effectively addressing the other problems of social life. A society in complete or near chaos cannot address any social problem effectively, however serious that problem may be. This is like stealing from a building's foundation to add more floors to the top. A very well-designed building can tolerate a bit of this type of activity without collapsing, but a *policy* of taking from the foundation to build a higher building increases the risk of collapse from the very first taking and ensures that a catastrophe will occur at some point if continued.

Second, if establishing and preserving social order actually prevents the effective pursuit of these other vital goals, we would seriously question the priority placed on social order. To the contrary, however, the achievement of social order based on libertarian precepts of justice and the rule of law makes it possible for other institutions to pursue other goals without violating the constraints imposed by these precepts of justice. Indeed, a consequentialist analysis would reveal such institutions to be far more capable of addressing these other problems than any known alternative, especially institutions that override natural rights.

The natural rights method I have described, with its consequentialist component, allows the theoretical possibility that, in extreme and abnormal instances, exceptions are justified. I am skeptical that any exception to the regime of justice and the rule of law is necessary or prudent, but on this issue, reasonable people in the classical liberal tradition have and will continue to differ. Indeed, libertarians can be distinguished from their classical liberal fellow travelers by the former's deep skepticism about making exceptions. Although I believe this skepticism is warranted, it is based as much on past experience with the consequences of recognizing exceptions—especially the inability to confine exceptions to the exceptional—as it is on any first principles about natural rights, each of which have various exceptions already built in.

Finally, while a commitment to moral "neutrality" per se is not a tenet of libertarianism, a libertarian natural rights approach is operationally neutral among the many alternative ways to pursue happiness that are consistent with the basic requirements of social order. Because libertarianism prohibits conduct that violates natural rights, it will unavoidably, but only incidentally, prohibit some actions that are individually bad and will bar using force to require some acts that may well be good. Persons who wish to pursue happiness by violating the rights of others may be condemned for acting badly or immorally (that is, contrary to the good), but they may be forcibly coerced only because they are acting unjustly (that is, contrary to natural rights). Persons who wish to see their comprehensive moral vision implemented may do so, but only by "just" means that do not violate the side constraints on action identified by libertarian natural rights.

Conclusion:
How Libertarianism Differs From Conservatism

In contrast with the moralism of traditional conservative or neoconservative approaches, libertarians often sound legalistic. The analysis presented here helps explain why. Libertarian political theory transcends different conflicting approaches to morality. Unlike moral or religious theorists, libertarians, qua libertarians, are not seeking a universal and comprehensive answer to the question of how persons ought to behave. Rather, Libertarians seek a universal answer to the question of when the use of force is justified. Libertarians, qua libertarians, do not deny that a more ambitious comprehensive morality exists; they merely deny the political claim that immorality, standing alone, is an adequate justification for the use of force by one person against another. In contrast, many conservatives assume, usually implicitly, that force is justified whenever human conduct is found to be bad or immoral. Libertarianism is much more modest, but for good reason. Libertarians seek a political theory that could be accepted by persons of diverse approaches to morality living together and interacting in what Hayek called the Great Society.

Any political theory that would enforce all moral norms would immediately confront radically different views of morality held by others in the same civil society. Enforcing morality would require the attainment of political power by those with one moral approach and the forcible suppression of any who disagree. Naturally, many of those who dissent will resist. In this way, a war of all against all is likely to result as each proponent of a comprehensive moral view seeks to attain a coercive monopoly of power over others and to avoid others attaining a monopoly of power over them. The situation is exacerbated when the source of morality comes solely from a religious faith, which is not shared by all, rather than also from reason.

A libertarian natural rights approach undertakes to identify, largely successfully, a law that is common to all: prohibiting murder, rape, theft, and so on. Whatever their moral differences, few purveyors of a comprehensive moral vision, whether religiously based or not, or even most criminals for that matter, disagree about the injustice of these types of acts. These people simply grant themselves an exemption from these principles when pursuing what they regard as higher moral or religious ends.

Traditionalist or social conservatives, neoconservatives, and those on the Left who seek to impose by force their conception of the good neglect the *problem of power*—an exacerbated instance of the twin social problems of knowledge and interest.[27] Once the use of power is legitimated on any ground, its use must somehow be limited to this ground and not be extended beyond. Using power raises the cost of erroneous judgment by imposing greater burdens on those who are

27. See Barnett, *The Structure of Liberty*, pt. III.

mistakenly victimized; once created, the instruments of power can be captured to serve the interests of those who wield it rather than to serve the end of justice. And, as we have just seen, once the use of force is accepted as a legitimate means for imposing on dissenters a comprehensive morality, then each group has the incentive to capture the institutions employing powers of coercion to wield these institutions against those who hold different moral views and to keep these institutions from being captured and used by others against them.

For all these reasons, libertarians contend that we must place conceptual and institutional limits or constraints on the exercise of power, including the power to do good or to demand moral or virtuous conduct. For comprehensive moralists of the Right or Left, using force to impose their morality on others might be their first choice among social arrangements. Having another's comprehensive morality imposed upon the moralists by force is their last choice. The libertarian minimalist approach of enforcing only the natural rights that define justice should be everyone's second choice—a compromise, as it were, that makes civil society possible. And therein lies its imperative.

CHAPTER FOUR

Libertarianism and Character

Richard A. Epstein

Political Rights and Moral Theory

The topic of this chapter is the relationship between libertarian theory and the development of individual character. To set the stage very quickly, I note at the outset that the general principles of Libertarian thought are powerful because of their simplicity: respect individual autonomy, enforce property rights, respect private contract. Classical liberal theories conceive of a somewhat larger role for the state, which has the power to impose taxes, condemn property, manage common pool resources, and limit the power of monopoly. For the purposes of this chapter, however, the differences between these two theories are relatively unimportant because the focus is on those personal obligations that individuals have to their fellow citizens, not on the legal mechanisms of the enforcement of those obligations.[1] Hence, although these differences will be noted when relevant, I shall only

My thanks to Eric Murphy for his usual redoubtable research assistance.

1. For a more detailed discussion of my views, see Richard A. Epstein, *Skepticism and Freedom: A Modern Case for Classical Liberalism* (Chicago: University of Chicago, 2003), 1–8.

stress the similarities between the two schools of thought. For convenience's sake, I therefore use these two terms interchangeably, unless otherwise noted.

Libertarian thought, broadly conceived, has little to say about the character and motivations of ordinary human beings. To be sure, libertarian thought develops a moral system insofar as it works with concepts of justice and injustice, right and wrong. But as a moral theory, its sole office is to establish the proper set of legal relationships between individuals. It is not, in any sense, an effort to identify the mainsprings of human conduct, to guide individual choices, or to prescribe whether people can be generous or stingy, gregarious or taciturn, impulsive or reflective. Indeed, it would be a mistake of major proportions to assume that legal rules are a dominant force in shaping individual character; family, school, and church are much more likely to be powerful influences. The people who run these institutions will use their influence to advance whatever conceptions of the good they hold, no matter what the state of the law. The generous person will continue to be generous even (and perhaps because) the law does not impose an obligation of generosity.

Within this large set of social and personal influences, libertarian thought sets rules that, in many ways, moral theorists would treat, at most, as moral minimums. The legal enterprise sets some outer boundaries on individual choice and then lets each person decide what moral principles to follow within those bounds. Keep your promises, don't assault your neighbor, and don't trespass on your neighbor's property are not standards that exhaust the list of behaviors that anyone would attribute to those individuals who are worthy of our admiration and respect. Public service, compassion, integrity, spirituality, conviction, imagination, patience, moderation, understanding, helpfulness, and a thousand other traits seem to gain widespread moral approbation and show the hollowness of insisting that efforts to treat various forms of moral judgment are invariably subjective or arbitrary. Any stress on legal theory should not, however, be used to conceal the importance of these characteristics in forging stable communities and organizations. In some cases, lawyers and economists do try to understand how these elements work. One notable example in this direction is Truman Bewley's perceptive study of workplace morale.[2] But, in general, the purpose of libertarian theory is to identify the proper rules for social organization, which leads libertarians to stress economic arguments about legal arrangements.

Great legal thinkers have often been criticized because of their unwillingness to plumb the depths of human emotion—that is the heart of John Stuart Mill's critique of Jeremy Bentham in his famous essay.[3] But there is, I think, a certain cold logic that holds that some separation of law from morals works on both sides of the relationship. To be sure, the basic prohibitions against murder, theft, and trespass rest on a strong sense of right and wrong conduct of the sort that requires the backing of legal sanctions. For huge areas of human inquiry, however, it is possible to identify other vital issues in which decisions cannot be reduced to workable legal standards. Here is one quick example: A look at the qualifications for the office of president under the U.S. Constitution reveals that the president (today) must be born a citizen of the United States, must be at least thirty-five years of age, and must have resided in the United States for fourteen years.[4] Clearly, these requirements are groping, in some loose way, at issues of loyalty, maturity, and familiarity with the United States. But the Constitution sets out weak conditions relative to the seriousness of the inquiry. Everyone who thinks about choosing the president of the United States asks tough questions about health, age, leadership, knowledge, stamina, and a thousand other qualities. Yet no one thinks that these should be treated as formal requirements of the job subject

2. Truman Bewley, *Why Wages Don't Fall in a Recession* (New Haven, CT: Yale University Press, 1999).

3. John Stuart Mill, "Bentham," in *Essays on Politics and Culture*, ed. Gertrude Himmelfarb (Garden City, NJ: Doubleday, 1962), 85, 106–13.

4. U.S. Const. art. II, § 1.

to either administrative or judicial review. The Constitution's great genius lies in its minimalist view that the political judgment of electors must, in the end, guide the selection process, a point that holds even though the electoral college has never really functioned as a deliberative body.

So if the basic libertarian rules have little directly to say about character, why bother investigate the issue at all? The investigation is important because the rules of everyday life influence the characters of everyone, including ordinary citizens, the captains of industry, and public servants. That influence can be exercised in two distinct ways: First, the rules create subtle *incentives* toward the development of character traits that flourish within the system. Whatever kinds of behavior are rewarded will appear in greater abundance. Second, and of equal importance, the rules exert a powerful *selection effect*—those individuals who inherently have the traits most compatible with the legal regime are the ones who assume positions of influence and power within the system.

I have little doubt that there is a natural distribution of endowments in talents and temperaments that looks very much like that for height or lactose tolerance. People have different proclivities toward breaking promises, using force, lying, or helping the sick, just as they do for anything else. In dealing with both natural and social selection, it is the variance around the mean that matters. The choice of legal rules, therefore, is important because these selection effects tend to minimize the psychological dissonance between what people are asked or allowed to do in order to succeed and their comfort level in doing it. Quite simply, people who have the personality traits that match the legal norms are more likely to succeed at the business of life. This element of fit is perfectly evident with respect to occupational sorting in general and explains why my career as a bench scientist (no, talking is not a laboratory skill) aborted as soon as it began. The same forces that lead kids who enjoy math to become scientists or kids who like poetry to write jingles work as much in this context as they do in any other. In effect, the reward structures set up by the legal rules lead to shifts in relative fortunes in the short run, which in turn sets up a dynamic that works itself back into child rearing and education in the long run.

In dealing with this subject, it is important not to be utopian about the positive influences that libertarian rules of legal conduct have on individuals. There is a long tradition within the law that attacks the system because of its stubborn refusal to bridge the gap between moral and legal duties. To give but two examples: The common law has long taken the position that individuals have no duty to rescue strangers (as opposed to individuals with whom one is bound by status, such as parent and child, or contract, such as counselor and camper) who are in condition of imminent peril, even if the individuals could do so at little inconvenience or risk to themselves.[5] This position has been attacked on repeated occasions as revolting and barbaric and as promoting an excessive form of individualism inconsistent with social life. There are, without question, instances where the charges ring true, as in the famous case of Kitty Genovese, who was stabbed to death on a public street while several dozen people looked on, none of whom bothered to call the police because of fear of getting involved.

In the face of this grim example, the institutional defense of this rule starts with the position that when the conditions for easy rescue are satisfied, we can find few instances of individuals who will not lend a hand. Thus, most people will be more likely to assist in legal rescues if they know their own conduct will not be subject to legal challenges after the fact. It is worth noting that the legal system contains provisions that allow individuals to obtain restitution for their expenses in effectuating a rescue if they do so without the intention

---

5. See, for example, *Buch v. Armory*, 44 A. 809 (N.H. 1897), for the common-law view. For one of many critiques, see William L. Prosser, *The Law of Torts*, 4th ed. (St. Paul, MN: West, 1971), 341. "Such decisions are revolting to any moral sense," ibid., 341.

of conferring a gift.[6] Oddly enough, however, the case law offers virtually no instances of individuals seeking recompense under that provision, just as it offers, ironically, virtually no instances of lawsuits by people who have not been rescued in the few jurisdictions that have changed the common-law rule by statute. The risks of character deformation are real, but there is no clean way to remove them without creating other (and greater) complications.

In similar fashion, virtually all legal systems refuse to enforce gift promises, even when made with the greatest of solemnity.[7] In general, it is required that the promise be part of a bargain or be evidenced by a deed or some other form of writing. Yet, in most cases, these promises are respected; when they are not, it is often because of a change in background conditions (e.g., a rapid change in financial fortune) that might well excuse the performance of a gratuitous promise. Here again, one could chide the libertarian system of being neglectful of moral duties; but, in fact, the practical difficulties of implementation have proved sufficiently weighty that few jurisdictions have abandoned this basic rule, notwithstanding the enormous expansion of liability in other areas of contract law. As with the failure to rescue, the legal system appears to do enough for the moral issues simply by recognizing that both moral and legal duties exist, even as it does not seek to bridge the gap between them. No doubt, parents can teach their children the importance of helping those in need and keeping promises, all in the absence of legal compulsion. Indeed, the clear implication of these decisions is that the legal order depends heavily on social sanctions to enforce these moral obligations. After all, the very use of the phrases "imperfect obligation" or "moral duty" is an explicit rejection of any form of moral relativism with respect to rescue or promise keeping.

6. Restatement of Restitution, § 118.
7. See, for example, *Mills v. Wyman*, 3 Pick. 207 (Mass. 1825), defending the view that these promises should be a species of "imperfect obligations" not backed by the force of law.

Two Rival Frameworks

With these caveats in mind, it is important to take a more systematic view of the overall legal system in order to contrast the set of personality and character traits that are fostered in a libertarian universe with those that are fostered in the modern welfare state. It is useful to set out, in brief compass, what I think to be the hallmarks of the two systems in terms of the direct application of each to ordinary life.

Libertarian Entitlements

It is useful to elaborate on the key elements of the libertarian view (with classical liberal overtones allowing for the use of taxation and eminent domain powers) mentioned briefly in the introduction. All individuals have personal autonomy so long as they are of full age and competence. That autonomy carries with it the right to do as they please with their own bodies and natural talents, to enter into what associations they think fit, to choose what occupations and careers they desire, to marry (a term that carries a lot more freight today than it did a decade ago), and to raise and care for children. It also implies the right to acquire property—at least that property regarded as unowned in the state of nature—for their own use based on a legal regime that follows the strict principle of "prior in time is higher in right." It also denies a duty to rescue strangers, as noted earlier.

By the same token, the overall framework is more classical liberal than libertarian. It allows for the recognition of stable forms of common property, such as those developed for rivers and highways, and limitations on access to certain common pool resources, such as game and fish. It also allows for the collection of (proportionate) taxes and the enforcement of some antimonopoly legislation. The standard forms of private property are, in general, freely alienable, subject only to those restraints on alienation that are voluntarily assumed as part of the basic transaction. This same freedom also applies to transactions involving individual labor, in which the general rule is just as Hobbes stated it: the value of any good or service in exchange is that which the appetite of the buyer is content to give. Low transaction costs and the high velocity of transactions are crucial to the success of these voluntary markets.

This system also recognizes certain powerful universal duties *roughly* captured by Mill's harm principle,[8] which must be understood, quite consciously, as something narrower than a rule that treats one individual as harmed if he perceives himself as worse off by virtue of what another individual has done. In fact, the system embraces some exceptions that prove necessary for the idea of liberty (and the ownership of property) to survive at all. The moral intuition is that the definition of "harm" cannot be so broad as to allow the subjective offense taken by A to block the actions of B. This aggressive view of the harm principle replicates the most unattractive features of the Rawlsian minimax principle on a transaction-by-transaction basis. This principle states that legal changes should be made to improve the position of the worst off. If this is so, then, as applied to specific disputes, it gives a veto power to the person who thinks worst of what is about to happen. Every action could lower the happiness of another person (such as his worst enemy), but the liberty of any individual person cannot survive if judged solely in reference to the sensitivities of the one individual who is most upset with the action. This version of the harm principle is a recipe for social paralysis. Lawyers are at their commonsense best when they won't let this principle happen in practice. Thus, there is much sense in the common-law nuisance rule that holds that the extrasensitive plaintiff cannot shut down a church bell that has been in operation for a long time and has not bothered the community at large.[9] Much of the troublesome litigation under

8. John Stuart Mill, *On Liberty*, ed. Gertrude Himmelfarb (New York: Penguin Books, 1974) [1859].

9. See *Rogers v. Elliot*, 1 N.E. 768 (Mass. 1888).

the establishment clause, such as that over the use of the words "under God" in the Pledge of Allegiance, arises precisely because the one person most hostile to religion often dictates the pattern of behavior in public schools that is acceptable.[10] This outcome represents yet another example of the kind of interest group brokering that takes place in all public affairs, often on the somewhat overstated claims of "coercion" said to be imposed on those who choose not to participate in the particular activity.[11]

As these cases illustrate, the general fear that liberty will disappear beneath the harm principle leads to three basic qualifications of the principle, which I set out, but do not defend, here. The first is the principle that competitive injury does not count as harm, even if various unfair forms of competition (e.g., passing off and trade libel) do count because they involve the use of fraud and, occasionally, force. Second, new construction blocking a neighbor's view does not count as a harm to the neighboring owner. Finally, the mere fact that one takes offense to the conduct of another individual does not count as harm, no matter how distasteful the practice. This last principle does not require the state to limit certain forms of conduct in public places (e.g., nudity). These three harms, which are not counted in the harm principle, are routine occurrences, associated with greater gains on average to other individuals. I doubt whether a systematic social decision to ignore these harms counts as a Pareto improvement over a world in which each harm is duly recorded. Nonetheless, I suspect that summed over all times and all particular goods, the legal rule approaches that result: that is, I cannot conceive of anyone who is likely to be better off under any legal system that categorically treats these harms as actionable instead of irrelevant. But even if that stringent condition is not met, I have little doubt that the current regime offers huge net gains over a world that refused to accept these qual-

10. See Richard A. Epstein, *Toleration—The Lost Virtue, The Responsive Community* (forthcoming 2004).

11. *Elk Grove Unified School District v. Newdow*, 124 S. Ct. 2301 (2004).

ifications to the harm principle. For our purposes, I do not wish to emphasize the important differences between the libertarian and the classical liberal perspective; but I do insist that for this discussion the anarcho-libertarian position is off the table.

The Welfarist Position

It is also necessary to give a brief account of the welfarist position, which stands in opposition to the classical liberal view of the world. The word "opposition" is a tad strong, however, because there is little question that just as Franklin Roosevelt intended to save capitalism, so it is that the modern defender of the welfare state is not a hard-line Socialist who agrees with Prodhoun that all property is theft. Rather, in the usual formulation, modern welfarists accept large portions of the classical liberal system as a plausible point of departure for their own prescriptions. Stated otherwise, the position has a comprehensive theory of market failures that go far beyond the usual problems of pollution and public goods. Following are the key points of difference.

On matters of individual autonomy, the modern welfarists dispute the Lockean position that all individuals are entitled to the exclusive use of their own labor because the arbitrary distribution of natural talents cries out for some equalization of wealth, typically through a decidedly progressive tax. On matters of property acquisition, the welfarists express an uneasiness with the rules of occupation for land and capture for animals because of the arbitrary nature of the higher-in-time rule. On matters of contractual liberty, they do not think that the usual grounds of duress, fraud, nondisclosure, and incompetence exhaust the legitimate reasons for state intervention. They are willing to block voluntary transactions because of the alleged inequality of bargaining power between the parties and because of their deep conviction that strong informational asymmetries upset the contractual process.

Most concretely, modern welfarists tend to favor the full range of laws that limit individual freedom in employment by imposing rules that call for minimum wages or collective bargaining or that prevent people from refusing to hire or promote on grounds of race, sex, ethnicity, national origin, or increasingly, sexual orientation. Their definition of harm is likewise expanded—bad views or unpleasant neighbors become harms that are easily cognizable under the zoning law. Fair trade statutes may properly provide strong protection against effective economic competition. Ironically, it appears that the first-in-time rule, to which they are skeptical with respect to the acquisition of property, has some claim for the prior acquisition of market position—that is, the right to do business with other people—at least if the claimants are individuals or firms within the jurisdiction. Likewise, *selective* forms of offense justify public intervention, such as the revulsion at racial discrimination but not, of course, same-sex marriages. It is obviously dangerous to generalize across the entire legal world, because these new grounds for intervention are often resisted in individual cases. Some zoning laws are thought to discriminate against members of minority groups. In addition, free trade in the international arena has received an admirable boost from, for example, the *New York Times*, which has yet to see a welfare or education program that it is unwilling to expand. But even so, this snapshot summary does capture a good deal of what goes on. How then do these two worldviews translate into differences in character development?

Character Formation as a Response to Legal Rules

As noted earlier, the basic incentive mechanism of legal norms is that individual character traits that receive positive payoffs from the norms will tend to grow relative to those that do not. People will develop those traits that promise positive returns. At the same time, a social form of Darwinian selection will favor individuals whose personality types reduce the stress between how they think and feel and the behaviors to which the legal system attaches positive (or negative) payoffs. Point by point, how does this all play out?

Autonomy and Redistribution

The standard libertarian position treats individuals as the owners of their own labor, which they can use as they like, as long as they do not interfere with the like liberty of others. The willingness to work at one's productive peak is necessarily enhanced by the knowledge that one can keep what he has earned, without being forced to share it with strangers. In turn, those strangers no longer have an incentive to hold back from doing work of their own in the hope that their passivity will create some entitlement against their more productive peers. The willingness to sluff off will often require individuals to conceal their true intentions so that dissimulation becomes a private advantage even though it is a public liability.

Note that this observation is *not* an argument against all taxation, only against taxes that are heavily and overtly redistributive. In contrast, under the libertarian (or at least classical liberal) view of the world, the taxes imposed under the benefit theory should neither reduce the incentive to engage in hard labor nor create envy or resentment between neighbors. The taxes in question are all designed to provide individuals with goods that they could not acquire in voluntary transactions. Properly executed, the benefit received from the taxes paid is worth more than the taxes paid for each person. In effect, therefore, every worker in the tax world has a *better* incentive to create than anyone who goes without these needed public goods. Without the tax, a person's return from labor could be X. With the taxation, it is $X - T + B$, which is a higher return on labor so long as $B > T$. The proportionate tax requirement used to make the benefit theory operational counters the ability of any faction to tilt the incidence of taxation toward other groups and away from its own. The strong requirement that the taxes go to public goods limits the ability to skew the benefit and, with it, openings for factional advantage. The form of the tax, however, does not limit the total level of public expenditures, which could be set as high or as low as the fundamental purposes required by the state—protection against force and fraud and the creation of infrastructure. People now have strong incentives to make honest revelations of their positions and to debate public issues candidly, knowing that they can benefit themselves only by helping others equally. The rules reward hard labor and honest labor. By creating win/win situations, no longer is there reason to engage in divisive rhetoric that attacks success as though it were greed, or worse. Public dialogue is improved because the gains from demagoguery are reduced. Thus, the proper legal rules, including those on taxation, create an optimal incentive structure for productive labor.

Once the welfarist's view that all individuals' talents should be treated as shared goods is accepted, the entire system of public discourse is altered for the worse. Each person is viewed as having an inchoate lien on the labor of everyone else, so that it nows pays to cut back production and plead poverty. In this environment, the tax system does not enhance individual productivity; instead, it becomes a powerful and serious barrier against the system's development. As long as the prospect of having others take care of a person exists, it reduces the need and the willingness for family members to take care of each other. Not only is there less production, but also family structure becomes more fragile. Pervasive state support allows individuals to turn aside pleas for personal assistance on the ground that these are properly addressed, not to them as a matter of charity but to the state as a matter of obligation. The constant stress on redistribution spurs attacks on the rich on the ground that the earnings of the rich are illegitimate. Taxation is seen as a way to impose punishment on those who escaped their "fair share" of the tax burden, even if, as is probably the case, the flat tax redistributes wealth away from persons with very high income. The net effect is to encourage people to advance themselves by tearing down the achievements of others: a zero-sum game. This corrosive effect on public discourse breeds and rewards cynicism. It is a mistake to assume that classical liberal thought is indifferent to questions of public discourse and morale. These ideas matter enormously, but typically they are best achieved by creating a sensible economic and political framework that rewards people for their successes and penalizes them for pretending to be victims.

Property

The rules for the acquisition of property count among the most controversial in the libertarian worldview. Why does the winner of the race to possession garner the property, to the exclusion of the rest of the world? The answer in part is that, systematically, we care less about who owns the property than about the fact that *"everything ought to have an owner."*[12] All property should be subject to an owner who is able to develop, consume, or trade the resource, that is, to use the resource in the most value-maximizing way. The legal rules are meant to establish a single owner with a minimum of fuss and bother. But what kinds of character does this rule reward?

On balance, it rewards those who are quick to spot opportunities and respond quickly to them. But it would be a mistake, I think, to regard this as a kind of character defect. Any individual who takes possession of land need not do so for himself but can do so in the name of a family, clan, or partnership.[13] The rules look much less egoistical in context of the overall framework than they do when standing alone. The rule in question does not have the same bedrock quality as do the rules that govern trade and harm. The clear recognition that possessory regimes can lead to the exhaustion of common pool resources often tempers the first possession rule by limiting what can be taken and how. If the overconsumption issue is solved by external constraint, then the traits of preparation, speed, and deter-

12. Henry Maine, *Ancient Law* (London: Oxford University Press, 1861), 213.
13. Ibid., 213–14.

mination, which determine success in individual races, are robbed of their negative associations. Indeed, we can say, more generally, that having to share common resources while recognizing the equal rights of access in others has exactly the opposite quality: it teaches people to work for private advantage within an overall common framework. The full panoply of rights is a mix of private and common property. It thus requires people to learn how to share the use of a sidewalk at the same time they tend to their own gardens.

I am hard-pressed to see any consistent set of character traits that emerge out of the rules governing the acquisition of private property through a system of first occupation, particularly today when the amount of unowned property that is subject to this rule is so small. The one large exception to this rule is the law of patents and copyrights, which strongly favors inventive and creative individuals by allowing them to garner rewards for their social contributions.

Contract

The impact on individual character (and social climate) of the legal rules that govern exchange is, on balance, much more profound. If the acquisition of unowned property is a rare and occasional event in modern society, then trade at all levels is an everyday occurrence. The parties in question are free to choose their trading partners and thus have strong incentives to develop reputations for reliability in order to induce others to do business with them. The larger the organization, the greater the risk that a single untoward incident could undo the power of the name or the brand, and the more diligent the steps that are taken to preserve them both. The long process of acculturation of new workers into firms is, in large measure, an effort to make sure that they understand how business is done by this or that firm. Internal to the firm is the constant mantra that X Company does not wish to get close to the line or be enmeshed in litigation for fear of what it will do to future business. The positive implications of these reputational sanctions do not require much elaboration.

Of course, more than reputation is at stake. One constant concern with contracting goes to the presumed level of competence of individuals who enter into transactions. The libertarian position identifies definable classes of individuals—the very young, the infirm, the insane—who suffer from transactional weaknesses that may require the appointment of a guardian with fiduciary duties to act on their behalf. But apart from this small but vital class of cases, it is evident that the practical competence of individuals of "full age and capacity" differs strongly across individuals. Yet nothing whatsoever is done to make the legal rules track the gradations in ability, be they large or small.

This stony indifference to matters of degree is the correct response because of the adaptive behavior it induces in ordinary individuals. It is a mistake of massive proportions to assume that the levels of transactional competence are invariant to the legal regime that governs trade. If individuals are told that they will always be relieved from their mistakes, they are that much more likely to make mistakes in the short run and that much less likely to take steps to improve their own competence in the long run. The prophecy of transactional incompetence becomes self-fulfilling. The entrenched set of low expectations leads to lower performance levels, which only intensify the pressure to introduce new measures of protection. The resulting vicious cycle retards individual self-improvement.

The situation, moreover, is made worse because social judgments of individual competence can never be made in a vacuum. All trades involve two parties, and any willingness to allow for the incompetence of one individual necessarily redounds to the inconvenience of the other, whose risks are necessarily increased. In the simplest model, suppose that we grant an option to any person who can claim incompetence or error to pull out of the deal before the other side has expended resources on it. Functionally, that rule is the equivalent of a free option (for a skillful trader perhaps) to one party that shifts but does not increase the value in the deal. These effects are felt not only after the deal is entered into. They will also be understood before so that any party with that "free" option will receive less by way of consideration than it could have received if able to bind itself in advance, which, however, the legal rules do not allow. If the losses exceed the potential gains from trade, the deal will simply collapse. Worse still, if both sides are given the statutory out, the risk of failure is still greater. The creation of these options, in effect, makes contracts more complex than they ought to be, which imposes greater burdens on those who are, in fact, less competent than others. It also gives incentives for people to feign incompetence because it works to their own legal advantage, which will increase the incidence of fraud and the propensity of people to commit it. Thus, the fraud will only drive honest people from the marketplace.

The standard legal response that holds parties to the "objective" meaning of contractual provisions represents one important way to stop this advantage-taking. This response has the added effect of making people be more explicit about their private intentions. It takes a certain degree of character to be up front with one's intentions, to honor one's promises, and to learn, without protest, from one's mistakes. But in the long run, doing so leads people to act with higher levels of competence than before so that the overall rate of contractual breakdown declines. This tough attitude toward business need not translate into situations where people are always in over their heads. It is possible for people to be competent about the limits of their competence and to hire agents to represent them. Just as it is easier to tell a good singer from a bad one than it is to sing, so it is easier to watch voluntary agents perform than it is to duplicate their efforts. Much of the elaborate system of the securities laws, for example, could be bypassed by the simple expedient of market segmentation: rather than have elaborate rules on full disclosure, tell people to buy into mutual funds that specialize in operating in an arm's-length world. Any rules that might work for amateurs only gum up the business for professionals. Once again, the demands of the unregulated (as to price and quantity) marketplace lead to the emergence of people with the self-knowledge and the character to respond to them.

All this is a far cry from the impact of government regulation on voluntary transactions. Let me begin with simple two-party contracts—employment, service, rental, or whatever—where the libertarian principle rightly announces that people have the right to choose their trading partners and to trade with them on whatever terms and conditions they see fit. The import of this proposition is that the state has to have strong reasons to either block or to require an ordinary transaction. In the absence of strong monopoly power, this proposition negates the appropriateness of *any* generalized antidiscrimination rule that forbids parties from trading on certain grounds. In this case, the key insight of the libertarian position is that relationships of trust can only emerge from transactions that are voluntary at their inception. Frequently, the choice of trading partners is, in practice, more important to the success of a deal than the particular terms of the engagement. A high level of trust reduces the need for contractual detail or contractual monitoring. In a successful relationship, neither side becomes reluctant to depart from the basic understanding because each fears losing the hefty long-term gains from a continuing relationship. Indeed, if each side gains some affection for the other, then loyalty cements relationships that self-interest has created. Contract formation breeds contract formation. Even at-will relationships are stabilizing via this bonding mechanism. Each side knows, moreover, that pushing too hard on the deal might induce the other side to walk, as the element of parity and trust dissolves.

The legal system backs up these cooperative sentiments by a swift and sure enforcement of basic terms and by awarding legal sanctions against various forms of fraud or opportunistic behavior. Contract terminations are purely social and business decisions; contract breaches are not. The interplay of nonlegal and legal sanctions helps the parties work in harmony for long periods, even in the face of unforeseen contingencies.

This model of trust, and the character development it encourages, will not work when the state limits the choice of trading partners so that the deal itself is perceived as a win/lose relationship from the outset. One vivid illustration arises under rent control statutes, in which the tenant is entitled by law to remain in possession under a lease (whose terms are set by the state at a below-market rate) even after its expiration. Under this regime, landlords and tenants alike have enormous incentives to game the system by noncooperative behavior. Tenants can damage common areas or be uncooperative in other ways because they do not fear being tossed out at the end of the lease, or even for cause during its term. Landlords often will take drastic action—including the disruption of water, electricity, and heat—to drive tenants out. New York City teems with stories of landlords hiring derelicts to haunt their buildings to persuade their tenants to vacate. The New York rental market has an embedded culture of pitched battles between landlords and tenants, driven by the two mechanisms of character formation mentioned earlier. Any reasonable landlord will be played for a patsy. Prospective entrepreneurs who have no stomach for rough tactics choose another line of business. Neither of these selection traits are at work in Chicago, where leases turn over peacefully and without incident twice a year. The rents are always close to market value, so there is no huge prize from misconduct equal to the capitalized value of the difference between the market and statutory rents. Chicago has no landlord/ tenant horror stories. Far from wanting to throw tenants out, most landlords are happy to renew leases at market rates to avoid the costs of reletting, with its attendant uncertainties, and to extend small favors (letting servicemen in, fixing drains, etc.) to preserve a relationship that both sides want.

There is a lesson here: The common view that strong protection of property and contract leads to some form of "possessive individualism" under which greed is paramount gets the story exactly backward. Voluntary transactions require one to woo others with promises, not to intimidate them with threats. The mutual ability to withdraw from negotiations introduces a level of cooperation on both sides. The ability to divide gains from long-term voluntary arrangements depends on this cooperation. The ability to succeed in a rent-controlled world depends on the opposite traits.

Thus far, I have stressed the protection that rent control affords sitting tenants in the renewal of leases. But suppose some unit falls vacant so that the system now operates as a standard form of price control that sets rents below market rates. The standard economic theory duly predicts that the resulting shortages will induce hordes of disgruntled customers to resort to bribes, connections, and guile to surge to the head of the queue. To be blunt, price (and wage) regulations are incubators of institutionalized fraud, as individuals recharacterize their transactions to avoid the sting, issue phony receipts, or rely on kickbacks or side payments. Once again, the maneuvering in this regulatory environment is uncongenial to people who like open and aboveboard arrangements. Again, one of two things happens: either the virtuous exit the field as persons of more dubious temperaments stream in or the virtuous master the devious ways of the underground economy to survive and thus lose their virtuous qualities.

The same regrettable patterns of behavior emerge when legal regulations suspend the ordinary right to hire and fire so that termination must be "for cause" and never be at will. Here, of course, private parties are free to use for-cause arrangements; but usually they do not, preferring to adopt rules that preserve the right to terminate that is perhaps conditional on some lump-sum payments. But state regulators and judges are often drawn to for-cause rules for unjust dismissal as a nifty way of preserving markets on the one hand—they are less intrusive than rent control laws—while countering egregious or irrational conduct on the other. Chief among these rules are the antidiscrimination laws that preclude employment decisions—hiring, firing, promotion, wages—based on the race, sex, ethnicity, age, disability, or sexual orientation of workers. Similar rules under the National Labor Relations Act prohibit dismissal or lesser sanctions made with antiunion animus. These rules do *not* require continued business, as rent control statutes do, because they allow employers to refuse to do business with employees for legitimate reasons.

The proponents of for-cause rules start from a moral base of ruling out hateful motives that have no place in commercial life. The hope is that these legal rules will induce people to put aside their biases and preconceptions in dealing with others. But the approach routinely fails. First, it overestimates the ability to determine which actions are done with improper motives. All too often, employers are unable to articulate their valid reasons to outsiders who lack situational knowledge. Second, the rule underestimates the ability of workers to identify with more favorable employers, which is only hampered by the implicit barriers to entry that the antidiscrimination laws supply. Third, the entire system encourages a culture of victimhood in which people find that they can improve their legal position by loudly announcing their inability to succeed on the strength of self-reliance. This defeatist attitude sends exactly the wrong signal to young people entering the workforce by understating their chances for success in an open market. This wrong information, in turn, could lead them to lower their expectations or their investments in human capital, leading to a reduction in long-term economic growth and personal well-being. Fourth, the for-cause regime violates the liberal principle of mutual advantage through trade. In unregulated labor markets, individuals on the social periphery have two effective means of getting a foot in the door: they can offer their services at bargain rates, or, as still happens in many jobs, they can start out as unpaid interns. The untrammeled ability to fire workers if they do not work out increases the odds of someone being hired in the first place. The whole emphasis is on lowering barriers to entry, not in setting up protections that will entrench the first workers to make it over the barriers. The sorting mechanism allows for rapid advancement of high-performance workers because no employer has the incentive to retain the weak workers in this high-risk group.

For-cause rules and antidiscrimination norms usher in manifest changes. The latter rules make it hard for high-risk candidates to underbid their rivals. The employer is now in the unhappy situation of having to pay the same wages to two candidates who differ on some important particular that is observable to him but not to the regulator. To overtly offer, say, a high-risk black candidate a lower wage than a low-risk white candidate is asking for trouble, even if an employer could offer differential wages to two candidates of the same race. The result is, therefore, either evasion to avoid hiring the unwanted worker or entering into a relationship from which the employer does not expect to profit. At this point, the employer's major goal is to find ways to cut back surreptitiously on his commitment in order to induce a "voluntary" quit by an unwanted worker. Incidents of underhanded conduct, in turn, give rise to the stronger enforcement of the law, which only further complicates matters. But turnabout is fair play, for the employee who is in a quasi civil service position has strong incentive to shirk on the job, knowing that the availability of legal remedy will deter dismissal or demotion. Employers look for pretexts to refuse to hire or to dismiss unwanted workers. Some workers go so far as to set up wrongful dismissal actions, by acting in covert ways that irritate an employer but that will not be seen to justify discharge. Each side has ample incentive to game the other because the relationship would not be viable in the absence of external constraints. To make matters worse, all employers must document dismissals or lesser sanctions with defamatory material. No one wants to say that all relationships are tainted by these extrinsic situations, when obviously most employment relationships are voluntary even under the current law; but the legal rules lead to forced associations that offer reasons for dissimulation that are not built into voluntary arrangements.

To be sure, no one doubts that for-cause rules could do some good in some cases of arbitrary dismissal. The net benefit is likely to be small, however, given the vital countervailing force that employers have little incentive to hurt themselves in order to hurt their employees. At the very least, cold-blooded self-interest limits the dangers of caprice, and any dislocation is mitigated by the greater ease of recontracting under an at-will system. The for-cause and the antidiscrimination regimes are different from the at-will situation in that not only do they tolerate various forms of opportunism, but also they literally invite it. Because the contracts that are formed under state compulsion are unwanted, it leads some tough-minded employers to practice covert discrimination in which they would not engage under an open-market system. To repeat, the successful contract requires a system of voluntary cooperation, which in turn brings out the ability to cooperate in the people who work under it. Any system that forces association has built-in incentives for various forms of fraud and social intrigues. Once again, the new rules encourage employers to be more devious and suspicious, and the people that thrive in the long run under this system are the ones with these negative traits. Thus, the legal rule shapes the character of the regulated parties.

Harms

The definition of "harm" used by the tort system also affects character formation. The prohibitions of the libertarian system are against aggression and deceit. In contrast, the broader definitions of "harm" that operate in the modern legal system have more or less the same consequences. Treating competitive harm as an actionable wrong has the unfortunate trait of encouraging people to rail against foreigners for stealing American jobs, often with racist overtones that would be intolerable in the domestic context. Similar hostilities arise in organizing campaigns in domestic labor markets. Epithets such as "scab" and "yellow dog" show the depth of the anticompetitive sentiment against foreigners in domestic labor markets. This sentiment is not remedied by rules that require forced association. Competitive harms

are ubiquitous, and the willingness to treat these as legitimate grievances helps people who prefer vilification and intrigue over productive
labor. At root, the demand to be rid of competition is merely a dis-
guised claim for redistribution through regulation, with the same consequences as redistribution through taxation.

Similar patterns of behavior exist in connection with the second
form of harm: the blockage of view or, indeed, any loss of ostensible
neighborhood amenities. These harms transcend the common law of
nuisance, with its emphasis on physical invasions, as supplemented by
reciprocal obligations of lateral support between neighbors. All too
often, zoning boards are lobbied to restrict land use by fiat, even
though the benefited landowners would never consider purchasing
that needed protection by voluntary restrictive covenant. As with labor
competition, it is commonplace for outsiders, especially foreigners, to
be most vulnerable to local political intrigue—"Want a permit for the
site, then sell to a local." Of course, people develop the character
traits to match the new set of opportunities; bigotry and jealousy have
broader areas in which to flourish. The sensible form of land use
regulation typically requires individuals to bear the same burdens as
they wish to impose on their neighbors or to pay compensation for
any disparity. In that case, the emphasis would be on an accurate
assessment of losses that is internalized either through the operation
of the rule or the payment of compensation. There would be no
incentive for intrigue under a robust system of property rights.

This same pattern applies, even more so, with respect to any legal
system that recognizes the subjective offense taken to the actions of
others as a cognizable source of harm. Yet, if personal offense triggers
a legitimate individual or group response, all bets are off. To the
libertarian, mere offense never generates an entitlement to stop the
activities of a person. The rational response to maximize private welfare is to be more tolerant of what others do. You know that you
have no right to stop them, so just relax. Or if agitated, try to persuade
individuals, one by one, to avoid the practices of which you disap-

prove. Legal rules cannot stop or slow down certain forms of action that are nonetheless amenable to social pressure. It is all relatively civilized. However, if the category of harms *contra bones mores* becomes a legitimate ground for public intervention, then the incentives are reversed. To be indifferent as to whether X wears a headpiece, or engages in premarital or homosexual or polygamous arrangements, diminishes your right to control the conduct of others. But working yourself up into a white heat only helps justify criminal sanctions or the denial of state licenses.

The game, of course, is one that both sides can play. Hence, one of the common justifications for the antidiscrimination laws is a different version of the principle of *contra bones mores*—namely, that "I don't want to live in a society in which individuals can discriminate on the basis of race or pay below some minimum wage, and so on." It is on this point, without question, that one finds the sharpest disagreement between the libertarians on the one hand and the traditional conservatives on the other. This gap can be bridged, at least in part, by traditional conservatives, who urge their position from their pulpits and platforms without seeking to institute their beliefs on moral questions as a matter of law. In some cases, however, the opposite takes place, as with the current efforts to pass a Family Marriage Act, which reads as follows:

> Marriage in the United States shall consist only of the union of a man and a woman. Neither this Constitution, nor the constitution of any State, shall be construed to require that marriage or the legal incidents thereof be conferred upon any union other than the union of a man and a woman.

My concern here is not with the difficult questions that remain with respect to the religious recognition of same-sex units or the payment of various forms of federal, state, and employer benefits. Rather, it is with the basic conception that deep offense offers sufficient normative warrant for the use of coercion against others. My concern here runs in both directions, because the opposite set of moral beliefs has led many to favor the use of state coercion to make sure that religious organizations accept gay groups into their activities, notwithstanding the tension with the organizations' Biblical beliefs. It is not my purpose to arbitrate the moral dispute between the two sides; instead, I argue against the articulation of inconsistent, all-purpose moral agendas that invite pitched public battles as to the rights and wrongs of conduct. There is real danger in anyone using any extended version of Mill's harm principle to impose impose his or her visions of the world on those who disagree. In so doing, the imposer spawns the kinds of hatreds and resentments that can lead to genuine cultural wars and make it harder to hew to the grand principle of live-and-let-live. The libertarian definitions of harm do not make individuals of perfect virtue, but they do hem in various forms of rhetorical excess, which raises the influence of the contentious among us.

Regulation

In closing, I want to mention one other area in which the modern welfarist solutions have contributed to the breakdown of civic discourse and character development. I am referring to the interaction between the weak eminent domain law and the strong protections for freedom of speech that defines U.S. Supreme Court doctrine. The fundamental source of weakness in the takings law lies in the sharp discontinuity between outright physical dispossession, which purports to supply full compensation, and "mere" restrictions on land use, which call for no compensation because they leave the owner in possession. I ignore all complications about consequential damages, such as the costs of conducting the move or any loss of good will, which are not covered in the physical takings cases.

Think of a simple grid in the shape of a tic-tac-toe board in which the eight squares along the rim have been built up: what activities should take place on the center square, which is privately owned? If the proposal is to purchase that plot for use as a park, at least a majority of the surrounding blocks will conclude that the enhanced value of their own lands because of the park is greater than the taxes needed to acquire it. The only speech that will be welcomed by the outer eight is that which contains truthful information about the trade-off. The likely outcome is that the property will be condemned only if the cost of the government action, including the costs of its administration, is less than the value received. There are no gains from hyperbole, and there is a stubborn resistance to its use.

This debate will follow different lines if the only point at issue is whether the owner of the central tract will be restricted in his development rights at little or no cost to the other eight owners. In this case, free speech will contribute to the downward cycle, for it is easy to form winning alliances by stressing the value to those who take while ignoring or belittling any losses to the owner whose property is taken. The wrong prices established under the takings law now shape the dialogue in ways that work antithetical to the overall good. The situation gets no better when the example is made more concrete. The target of land use restrictions may be singled out in the heat of battle, thereby increasing the risk of imposing differential regulations on members of racial or ethnic minorities. The price constraint embodied in the just compensation requirement works as an antidote to these exaggerated statements, which should improve the overall character of public discourse. The feedback mechanism found in compensation should increase sober deliberation, which in turn increases the fraction of responsible individuals in public debate.

Conclusion

One central element of the welfarist position is that even if systems of strong property rights and limited government fare well on narrow economic grounds, they do much worse on other criteria that stress the formation of individual character, social cohesion, and individual rights. This conclusion is false. Forcing private individuals to go to the market and forcing the state to use its eminent domain power introduce a level of discipline that helps form self-reliant individuals and promote honest public debate. Dispensing with these constraints, however, creates a different mix: it substitutes self-pity for self-reliance; it encourages a culture of excuses; it invites dissimulation and distrust; it spawns factional struggle by encouraging factional intrigue as a substitute for honest labor. Everyone wants to get something for nothing. A political culture that lends respect to this attitude induces the wrong kinds of conduct on matters of markets or morals. The libertarian cannot figure out ways to make people wise or generous; people must find this for themselves. But sound political institutions can find ways to shield honest and generous persons from the machinations of others, thereby increasing the odds that desirable character traits will prove successful in the grubby business of life. And in law, as in medicine, an old refrain gains new urgency: *primum non nocere*—first do no harm.

PART III

Neoconservatism

CHAPTER FIVE

The
Neoconservative
Journey

Jacob Heilbrunn

The Neoconservative Conspiracy

The longer the United States struggles to impose order in postwar Iraq, the harsher indictments of the George W. Bush administration's foreign policy are becoming. "Acquiring additional burdens by engaging in new wars of liberation is the last thing the United States needs," declared one Bush critic in *Foreign Affairs*. "The principal problem is the mistaken belief that democracy is a talisman for all the world's ills, and that the United States has a responsibility to promote democratic government wherever in the world it is lacking."[1]

Does this sound like a Democratic pundit bashing Bush for partisan gain? Quite the contrary. The swipe came from Dimitri Simes, president of the Nixon Center and copublisher of *National Interest*. Simes is not alone in calling on the administration to reclaim the party's pre-Reagan heritage—to abandon the moralistic, Wilsonian, neoconservative dream of exporting democracy and return to a more limited and realistic foreign policy that avoids the pitfalls of Iraq.

1. Dimitri K. Simes, "America's Imperial Dilemma," *Foreign Affairs* (November/December 2003): 97, 100.

In fact, critics on the Left and Right are remarkably united in their assessment of the administration. Both believe a neoconservative cabal has hijacked the administration's foreign policy and has now overplayed its hand. Writing in the *London Review of Books*, for example, Anatol Lieven observed, "If the plans of the neocons depended on mass support for imperialism within the U.S., they would be doomed to failure. The attacks of 11 September, however, have given American imperialists the added force of wounded nationalism . . . strengthened by the Israeli nationalism of much of the American Jewish community."[2] "Long after the new fundamentalist thinking fades away," wrote G. John Ikenberry, "American diplomats will be repairing the damaged relations and political disarray it wrought."[3] Others see Bush as a mere puppet: "Now here we are on the downslope of 2003," wrote Alexander Cockburn in the *Nation*, "and George Bush is learning, way too late for his own good, that the neocons have been matchlessly wrong about everything."[4] "The neoconservatives . . . are largely responsible for getting us into the war against Iraq," observed Elizabeth Drew in the *New York Review of Books*.[5] George Soros, a Holocaust survivor, detected a "supremacist ideology" in the White House, while novelist Arundhati Roy warned that for the "first time in history, a single empire with an arsenal of weapons that could obliterate the world in an afternoon has complete, unipolar, economic and military hegemony."[6]

On the paleoconservative Right, Patrick J. Buchanan, editor of

2. Anatol Levin, "A Trap of Their Own Making," *London Review of Books* (May 8, 2003): 19.

3. G. John Ikenberry, "The End of the Neo-Conservative Moment," *Survival* (Spring 2004): 7.

4. Alexander Cockburn, "Behold, the Head of a Neocon!" *The Nation* (September 17, 2003): 8.

5. Elizabeth Drew, "The Neocons in Power," *New York Review of Books* (June 12, 2003): 20.

6. Arundhati Roy, "The New American Century," *The Nation* (February 9, 2004): 11.

the *American Conservative* and a longtime foe of the neoconservatives, asserted that Richard Perle, Paul Wolfowitz, Douglas Feith, among others, have formed an alien cabal intent on promoting a utopian, Bolshevik revolution around the globe. "President Bush is being lured into a trap baited for him by these neocons that could cost him his office and cause America to forfeit years of peace won by the sacrifices of two generations in the Cold War." These neoconservatives, Buchanan continued, "harbor a 'passionate attachment' to a nation not our own that causes them to subordinate the interests of their own country and to act on an assumption that, somehow, what's good for Israel is good for America."[7]

But where the paleoconservative and traditional conservative critics of neoconservatism part company with the Left is in their embrace of U.S. power. Instead of fearing American might, these critics admire it. However, they worry about squandering the country's power and are fond of recalling Edmund Burke's warning: "I dread our own power and our own ambition. I dread being too much dreaded."[8] Buchanan and George F. Will see neoconservatives, like the *Weekly Standard*'s William Kristol, as championing big government abroad. In essence, they see American humanitarianism abroad as the foreign policy equivalent of welfare: it puts hostile populations on the dole, while Washington pursues counterproductive social engineering schemes. The paleoconservatives even see the neoconservatives as imposters—renegade Trotskyists who have changed their outward political coloration several times but remain intent on a utopian, permanent revolution that expands U.S. power to every nook and cranny of the globe.

It's easy to see why conservatives, such as Buchanan, recoil at the neoconservative impulse, which began by criticizing radical tendencies

7. Patrick J. Buchanan, "Whose War?" *The American Conservative* (March 24, 2003): 5.

8. Edmund Burke, cited by Owen Harries, "Understanding America," at www.cis.org.au/Events/CIS lectures/2002/Harries 030402.htm..

inside the Democratic party before moving, decades later, firmly into the GOP camp. Neoconservatives have been allies, rather than long-standing members, of the GOP. They have traditionally prized independence more than allegiance to a particular political creed, though some, such as Richard Perle, remain members of the Democratic party, even as they travel in Republican circles. The close-knit circle of neoconservatives, from the American Enterprisse Institute to the Project for the New American Century, has fueled charges that they operate more like an underground cell than an intellectual movement.

But do neoconservatives really form a cabal that has suborned Bush and manipulated U.S. foreign policy on behalf of Israeli Prime Minister Ariel Sharon? Would the GOP be better off without the neoconservative persuasion that, in Irving Kristol's words, has taken as its mission converting the "Republican party, and American conservatism in general, against their respective wills, into a new kind of conservative politics suitable to governing a modern democracy"?[9] A look at the history of neoconservatism suggests that it would not.

Neoconservatism hardly has an unblemished record. It has, on more than one occasion, substituted polemical thrusts for sober analysis, alarmism for insight.[10] But it has formed, by and large, the intellectual brain trust for the GOP over the past two decades. Neoconservatism first earned prominence in the late 1960s, when liberal public intellectuals, such as Kristol and Daniel Patrick Moynihan, criticized the excesses of the welfare state and social planning. In the 1970s, neoconservatives added a foreign policy critique, condemning the flaccidity of the liberal response to communism after America's defeat in Vietnam. Although the neoconservatives argued that America may have gone astray in Vietnam, it was not the new international bad guy. Soviet expansionism, not American interven-

9. Irving Kristol, "The Neoconservative Persuasion," *The Weekly Standard* (August 25, 2003): 23.

10. For an eloquent critique, see Francis Fukuyama, "The Neoconservative Moment," *National Interest* (Summer 2004).

tionism, was the culprit for global ills. Israel, they maintained, should be defended from attacks by despotic Third World regimes masquerading at the United Nations as the conscience of humanity. For these beliefs, the neoconservatives were ridiculed by the liberal establishment: *Harper's* response was not untypical; it ran an article deriding the "Warrior Intellectuals," as leading Left thinker Frances FitzGerald dubbed Moynihan and others.

The neoconservatives were undaunted. The United States, they declared, needed to confront the Soviet Union whenever and wherever possible, emphasizing military power and human rights, particularly liberty for Soviet Jews to travel to Israel, Europe, and the United States. With the presidency of Ronald Reagan and the fall of the Berlin Wall in 1989, neoconservatives believed that their hawkish approach had been vindicated.

If the Soviet empire could be toppled, reasoned neoconservatives, so could Middle East totalitarianism. After September 11, neoconservatism offered a rationale for intervention abroad that Bush appeared to embrace. Neoconservatives argued that decades of terrorism emanating from the Middle East meant that an aggressive push for democracy and the unflinching use of U.S. military power had to take precedence. Iraq was supposed to be the test case for this new doctrine.

In recent months, however, neoconservatism has come into ill repute. It has not been possible to democratize Iraq as easily as many neoconservatives, such as Richard Perle, had predicted. *New York Times* columnist David Brooks, among others, confessed to succumbing to illusions about the malleability of Iraq and other foreign cultures. But a good case can be made that the problem with the Bush administration's policy in Iraq and elsewhere is not that it is dictated by neoconservatives but that it is not neoconservative enough. Had the Bush administration pushed more relentlessly and expended more resources in Iraq to secure democracy and human rights, it would not be flirting with a debacle in the Middle East. Whatever neoconservatism's pluses and minuses, for the GOP to follow the realist, let alone the paleoconservative, course would be a prescription for a crab-bed amoralism in international affairs and, ultimately, political impo-tence. Before neoconservatism becomes further enshrouded in myths by its adversaries on the Right as well as the Left, it might be useful to examine what neoconservatism has contributed to the conservative movement—and where it's headed.

The Origins of Neoconservatism

Perhaps one of the most potent myths about neoconservatism is that it is nothing more than Trotskyism dressed up as conservatism. This notion—that neoconservatism represents a kind of latter-day utopian, Bolshevism—has spread rapidly, even to the upper reaches of govern-ment, where Secretary of State Colin Powell's chief of staff, Larry Wilkerson, recently complained to, of all places, the magazine *Gen-tleman's Quarterly*: "I call them utopians. . . . I don't care whether utopians are Vladimir Lenin in a sealed train going to Moscow or Paul Wolfowitz. Utopians, I don't like. You're never going to bring utopia, and you're going to hurt a lot of people in the process of trying to do it."[11]

To repudiate such charges, a number of neoconservatives, includ-ing Joshua Muravchik, dismissed the notion that neoconservatism has anything to do with Trotskyism.[12] But this is not quite right. The development of neoconservatism certainly cannot be divorced from the ideological battles of the 1930s. Contrary to a number of histories, including John Ehrman's *The Rise of Neoconservatism*, neoconserva-tism is not simply a creature of the cold war that tried to maintain

11. Wil S. Hylton, "Casualty of War," *Gentleman's Quarterly* (June 2004): 227.
12. Joshua Muravchik, "The Neoconservative 'Cabal,'" *Commentary* (September 2003). See also Bill King, "Neoconservatives and Trotskyism," www.enterstage right.com, March 22, 2004. King maintained that "despite its current popularity, the 'Trotskyist neocon' assertion contributes nothing to our understanding of the origins, or nature, of neoconservatism."

cold war liberalism in the 1960s.[13] Its cold war had already begun in the 1930s, when Trotskyism served as a valuable way station on the road to all-out anticommunism after the Second World War.

Nothing dominated New York intellectual life more than disputes over communism in the 1930s. For Jews who had emigrated from Russia to the United States at the turn of the century, Communist doctrine was always appealing. The fellow-traveling writer Maurice Hindus published a study in 1927 called *The Jew as Radical*, which maintained that Jews had an innate propensity, dating back to their bibilical origins, for radicalism.

Although many Jews embraced the Soviet Union, the founding fathers of what would become neoconservatism—Lionel Trilling, Sidney Hook, and Elliot Cohen—did not. They viewed the Soviet Union as a degenerated workers' state and the intellectual outcast, Trotsky, with sympathy.

A signal event in strengthening the original neoconservatives' antipathy toward American Communists was a strike called for February 16, 1934, in New York to protest fascist Austrian chancellor Engelbert Dolluss's attack on Viennese communal tenements for workers. Madison Square Garden, which was filled with about 18,000 socialist trade union workers, was infiltrated by about 2,000 Communists, who marched in formation with banners and musical instruments. The Communists turned what was supposed to be a broad left-wing protest against fascism into a riot.

The socialist *New Leader* declared, "New York learned at first hand how it was that Hitler came into power in Germany when a vast demonstration of solidarity with heroic Austrian socialists . . . was turned into a dog-fight by the deliberate and planned actions of gangs that call themselves the Communist Party."[14] The fight in the Garden replicated the feud between Communists and Socialists in

13. John Ehrman, *The Rise of Neoconservatism* (New Haven, CT: Yale University Press, 1995).
14. "Madison Square Garden," *The New Leader* (February 24, 1934): 1.

Nazi Germany. Even as Hitler gained power, the German Communist party had slavishly followed Stalin's orders to battle, not the Nazis but the Social Democrats. Only one Marxist—Leon Trotsky—warned that this was a suicidal strategy. Not only did Trotsky warn of a European war, but also "Trotsky's Jewishness," wrote scholar Joseph Nevada, "came to the fore during the latter part of the 1930s. His abhorrence of Nazism appears to have extended beyond a deep-rooted antifascism. He was doubly articulate because of his racial origin; he clearly foresaw the imminent genocide of his coreligionists."[15]

Troksky's message resounded among intellectuals in the United States. In March 1934, *Modern Monthly* printed "An Open Letter to American Intellectuals," bemoaning that the Communists had wrecked a united front against fascism. The signers of the letter included Trilling and Cohen. The Communist party organ "New Masses" attacked "these loop-de-loopers from Zionism to 'internatioanlism': the Brenners, the Cohens, the Novacks, the Trillings. . . . They now imagine themselves to be Trotzkyies [sic], hence the declared enemies of the Communist Party use them for what they are worth."[16]

What was all the fuss about? It was, you might say, the first confrontation in the anti-Stalinist battle that would rage after World War II. Trotsky, as Alexander Bloom observed, gave young Jews a path out of the Jewish ghetto without committing the ultimate act of treason, which was to break with their parents' Socialist verities. Among those who embraced Trotskyism were Irving Kristol, Seymour Martin Lipset, and Gertrude Himmelfarb, as well as Albert Wohlstetter, who was a close friend of Sidney Hook's and who would play a pivotal role in grooming a generation of neoconservatives. At the City College of New York, these young intellectuals matched wits

15. Joseph Nevada, *Trotsky and the Jews* (Philadelphia: Jewish Publication Society), 5.

16. Cited in Alan M. Wald, *The New York Intellectuals* (Chapel Hill: North Carolina University Press, 1987), 63.

with the Stalinists. Kristol was a member of Max Schachtman's Workers' Party, or, to put it more precisely, of a faction inside the party called the "Shermanites."

For all their suspicion of Stalinism, these young intellectuals were lamentably blind to the danger represented by Nazism and the need for the United States to confront Germany. The main problem was that they were hostile to Roosevelt and mainstream liberalism. They denounced Stalin for conniving with Roosevelt rather than refusing to cooperate with him. Schachtman, who would groom neoconservatives such as Carl Gershman and Joshua Muravchik in the 1960s, by which time he had shed his Trotskyism, declared in the "New International" that the only issue of World War II was "who [is] going to get the major share of the swag. The blood stains all of their hands alike." In his view, "Hitler is not Attila" and Nazism represented "a stage in the development of capitalist society, the epoch of its decay."[17]

Kristol attacked Hook for supporting the war. According to Kristol, Hook was a demagogue: "In his near hysterical insistence upon the pressing military danger . . . we recognize not only a common academic reaction to events, but also an ominously familiar political weapon. It is the exact technique of the Communist-liberal coalition during the days of the Popular Front and Collective Security." Kristol added that "the war in Asia clarifies brutally the activating war aims of the United States, Britain, and the Netherlands as far as the vital questions of empire and freedom are concerned. Professor Hook busies himself with an abstract war against Hitler rather than handle the less attractive reality of a completely reactionary crusade against 'those yellow b—s.' It's always the other fellow's nerve."[18] Trotskyist Dwight MacDonald, in the February 1944 maiden issue of *Politics*, declared, "I think we can start out from the proposition that this war is not a

17. Max Schachtman, "Only Socialism Can Bring Peace and Freedom," *Labor Action* (February 28, 1944): 3.

18. William Ferry, "Other People's Nerve," *Enquiry* (May 1943): 5–6. (William Ferry was Kristol's Trotskyist cognomen.)

struggle between Good and Evil, or Democracy and Totalitarianism, but rather a clash of rival imperialisms."[19] As these passages suggest, it could be argued that Kristol, among others, was always wary of liberalism, whether he was on the Left or the Right.

The problem, of course, was that many early neoconservatives were blind to the great totalitarian threat posed by Hitler's murder of the Jews. A few were not. Wohlstetter, who with his wife, Roberta, sponsored numerous Jewish refugees, knew better. (He repeated this gesture during the Bosnian war, when genocide in Europe loomed again.) Alfred Kazin was also not blind. He famously wrote in the *New Republic* in 1943 that liberals, radicals, and conservatives alike were ignoring the tragedy taking place in Europe. Similarly, in the *New Leader*, the doughty Melvin J. Lasky condemned the passivity of the Roosevelt administration toward the murder of the Jews. And in *Labor Action*, Jessie Kaaren lamented that "there are at least hundreds of thousands, if not millions, that could be rescued in spite of the war and Nazi supervision if the Allied governments were to put into action the fine sounding phrases they devote themselves to, like those in the Atlantic Charter."[20]

By 1945, with the horrors of Europe impossible to overlook, everyone from Kristol to MacDonald was shedding the dogmas of Trotskyism for anticommunism. Anticommunism may even have become something of a psychological compensation for having missed the greatest tragedy of the twentieth century because everyone had been so preoccupied with debating the fine points of Marxist dogma.

But the New York intellectuals had indisputably learned about the dangers of Stalinism from Trotsky. In 1945, the view that the Soviet Union was a present danger was given weight and authority in an article by James Burnham in *Partisan Review*. In the article, called "Lenin's Heir," Burnham laid out what would become cold war anti-

19. Dwight MacDonald, *Politics* (February 1944): 1.
20. Jessie Kaaren, "Jews of Europe Face Doom," *Labor Action* (February 28 1944): 4.

Communist strategy, even before George F. Kennan had alerted Washington to the peril posed by the Kremlin. In his essay, Burnham observed that "most of us who developed an opposition to Stalinism from what we have regarded as the left were taught our first lessons by Trotsky." Burnham made the case that, far from being a mediocrity, as Trotsky had claimed, Stalin was a great leader who had laid the foundations for Soviet expansionism. Burnham grandiloquently declared, "Starting from the magnetic core of the Eurasian heartland, the Soviet power, like the reality of the One of Neo-Platonism overflowing in the descending series of the emanative progression, flows outward, west into Europe, south into the Near East, east into China, already lapping the shores of the Atlantic, the Yellow and China Seas, the Mediterranean, and the Persian Gulf . . . until it is dissipated in . . . the outer material sphere, beyond the Eurasian boundaries, of momentary Appeasement and Infiltration (England, the United States)."[21] The message was clear: Stalin had to be stopped. There could be no meaningful distinction between the Soviet leader and the Soviet Union itself. Both were a menace.

The Cold War

After World War II, it would have been entirely anachronistic to call Kristol, Hook, Lasky, and Cohen, the latter of whom was the founder of *Commentary* in 1945, neoconservatives. Conservatism was in disrepute; it was the province, by and large, of anti-Semites and kooks who continued to regard the New Deal as a species of domestic communism. But Kristol and Trilling, among others, were as wary of liberal orthodoxies as they were of right-wing ones.[22] Cohen, a bril-

21. James Burnham, "Lenin's Heir," *Partisan Review* (Winter 1945): 66–67.
22. Kristol pointed out that Trilling believed, "the liberal state of mind is reformist and humanitarian; a state of mind whose basis is snobbery, self-satisfaction, unimaginativeness. . . . The liberal flatters himself upon his intentions, 'and prefers not to know that the good will generate its own problems, that the love of humanity has its own vices and the love of truth its own insensibilities.' He is paternal and

liant editor, was particularly concerned to demonstrate in the postwar era that Jews could be relied upon. He wanted to show that not all Jews were Communists, which was, of course, true.

It was an understandable impulse. The Left was cracking up. The farther the Red Army reached into Europe, the more divided the American Left became. Anti-Communist liberals gathered around the Americans for Democratic Action (ADA), while progressives supported Henry Wallace for president. Former Trotskyists, such as Kristol, joined forces with the ADA, which was led by Arthur Schlesinger Jr. But far too little attention has been paid to the fact that many of the former Trotskyists did not become conventional liberals. They retained their suspicion of the weaknesses of conventional liberals. Anticommunism, Christopher Lasch somewhat overheatedly argued, "represented a new stage in their [the former Trotskyists'] running polemic against bourgeois sentimentality and weakness, bourgeois 'utopianism' and bourgeois materialism."[23] But it was certainly true that Kristol, Lasky, and others took a far more ideological approach to the cold war than did realist thinkers, such as Schlesinger, Walter Lippmann, and George F. Kennan. The split that would take place over Vietnam in 1968 was already dimly present in 1948. The future neoconservatives, who were more battle hardened than Schlesinger, were wary of liberalism's weakness in staring down communism. The ideological battles of the 1930s had prepared Kristol and others for a more ideological cold war. The fights over communism were now transported onto a larger canvas. Where they had previously been internecine feuds that occasionally spilled over into the public arena,

---

pedagogic, smug in the knowledge of his righteousness, and sure of the adequacy of his program. . . . An insidious cruelty is at work, in which all men are expendable in order to make a point." Irving Kristol, "The Moral Critic," *Enquiry* (April 1944): 22.

23. Christopher Lasch, *The Agony of the American Left* (New York: Vintage, 1966), 68.

the question of who was, and was not, a Communist, and who was, and was not, a fellow traveler acquired a new importance.

In a 1946 article in *Partisan Review*, for example, William Barrett attacked domestic traitors who wanted to appease the Soviet Union. He argued that liberals were "advocating a policy to sell out . . . millions into Stalinist slavery." "It is clear from this outline of their recent behavior," he noted, "that the 'liberals' are embarked upon nothing less than a policy of appeasement of Russia."[24] Kristol went one step further and pilloried liberals who had failed to denounce communism with sufficient ardor: "[T]here is one thing that the American people know about Senator McCarthy: he, like them, is unequivocally anti-Communist. About the spokesmen for American liberalism they feel they know no such thing. And with some justification."[25] To some degree, for Kristol, the cold war was about using the Communist issue as a wedge to attack liberals. It was the opposite of what Schlesinger believed—that communism from without, not within, was the real problem.

For all the ructions about communism in the early 1950s, much of the decade embodied a fairly placid consensus about America. It wasn't until the 1960s that the ideological battles resumed. Ironically enough, they were ignited by none other than the young editor of *Commentary*, Norman Podhoretz. Podhoretz rebelled at the notion that the United States embodied the good life. As he saw it, things were not so rosy as often depicted. The United States was decrepit, listless, moribund. What's more, the U.S. record in the cold war wasn't all that innocent. Podhoretz began publishing revisionist historian Staughton Lynd, who claimed that both sides were responsible for the cold war; William Appleman Williams, dean of the revisionists, claimed that Lynd was actually underestimating U.S. responsi-

24. William Barrett, *The Truants* (New York: Anchor Press, 1982), 244–49.
25. Irving Kristol, "'Civil Liberties,' 1952—A Study in Confusion," *Commentary* (March 1952): 229.

bility. Norman Birnbaum observed in 1962 that "Anti-Communism, as an intellectually respectable position, is ending."[26]

As the New Left drifted into violence, anti-Semitism, and black radicalism, however, neoconservatism emerged from its embryo. The extent to which neoconservatism is a movement that went from Left to Right has been greatly exaggerated. Podhoretz, who belonged to a younger generation, may have briefly flirted with radical ideas, but Kristol, Trilling, and others had always been wary of the weaknesses of the liberal Left in confronting totalitarian impulses. Since the late 1940s, they had been fairly consistent about their political views and didn't really change them all that much. To them, it seemed that on the home front liberals were once more succumbing to the threats and blandishments of the Far Left, as they had in the 1930s. Podhoretz had already written, in 1963, of "the insane rage that can stir in me at the thought of Negro anti-Semitism." Four years later, as Egypt massed forces in the Sinai desert and cut off Israel's access to the Suez Canal, black anti-Semitism began to reach a new high. After Israel won a sensational victory in the 1967 war, Jewish pride in the United States began to surge. By 1968, while addressing the Council of Foreign Relations, Podhoretz was accused by former John Kennedy speechwriter Theodore Sorensen of putting Israel's interests ahead of U.S. interests.

Far more volatile charges had already been leveled by black radicals and the New Left. In August 1967, the Student Nonviolent Coordinating Committee charged that Zionism was racism. At a National Conference for New Politics "Convention on 1968 and Beyond," which was held in Chicago over Labor Day weekend in 1967, radicals demanded a condemnation of Israel. Kristol later observed that "for 200 years Jews generally found their friends on the left. Now they find their enemies. . . . We have an interest—American

26. Norman Birnbaum, "The Coming End of Anti-Communism," *Partisan Review* (Summer 1962): 394.

Jews and Israelis—in preserving the status quo. Let us admit it, at least to ourselves."[27]

Perhaps the last straw for the budding neoconservatives was the assault on the schools and universities. Nowhere did the student revolt have more consequences for neoconservatism than at Cornell University in 1969, which was a hotbed of what had become known as Straussianism, after political philosopher Leo Strauss. In 1968, Straussian Nathan Tarcov, a recent graduate, approvingly recorded in the *Public Interest* that "Cornell did not have a revolution last year."[28] Cornell soon made up for lost time. On April 20, 1969, at least eighty members of the Afro-American Society marched out of the student union brandishing rifles. As future neoconservative Allan Bloom saw it, Cornell was reminiscent of Weimar, Germany, where servile liberals had capitulated to Nazi thugs. He declared that "the resemblance on all levels to the first stages of a totalitarian takeover are almost unbelievable."[29] For the students of Strauss, who had emigrated from Nazi Germany, the university administration capitulating to black student demands was a signal instance of liberal weakness. Strauss insisted on defending liberal values and of the need for an elite to inculcate those values through a demanding education in the great books. To Strauss, Israel was particularly important as an outpost of the West surrounded by moral enemies. In 1957, he even wrote a letter to the *National Review*, chastising it for being anti-Israel. Political Zionism restored the dignity of a people who remembered their heritage and stemmed the tide of the leveling of venerable differences; "it fulfilled a conservative function."

Much nonsense has been written about Strauss's supposed

27. Irving Spiegel, "American and Israeli Jews Reappraise Their Ties to the Left and Find They Are Now Tenuous," *New York Times,* 6 August 1972: 13.
28. Nathan Tarcov, "Cornell: The Last Four Years at Cornell," *Public Interest* (Fall 1968): 122.
29. Homer Bigart, "Faculty Revolt Upsets Cornell," *New York Times,* 25 April 1969: 1, 30.

attempt to create a fascistic elite intent on ruling the vulgar multitude. In truth, Strauss, like most neoconservatives, worried about a liberal failure of nerve in confronting the Soviet Union and in defending Israel. The central concern of neoconservatives was the encroachment of totalitarianism, whether in Europe or the Middle East. The pre-occupation was not with Israel as representing an outpost of the West. Were the United States to allow Israel to collapse, it would signal a fatal weakness in the larger struggle against Soviet totalitarianism.

The Political Influence of Neoconservatism

If neoconservatives were alarmed by what they saw as McGovernism, they were petrified by Richard Nixon and Henry Kissinger's embrace of détente with the Soviet Union. It could be argued that no one did more to turn neoconservatism into a potent political force than did Kissinger. Like Strauss, Kissinger was an émigré from Germany, but he drew radically different lessons. Where Strauss believed it necessary to confront totalitarian regimes, Kissinger thought it necessary to cut deals with unsavory leaders and work out an accommodation. Indeed, Kissinger was a declinist who believed that the United States had to manage its foreign policy twilight.

Neconservatives, such as Moynihan and Podhoretz, disagreed with Kissinger. But until the early 1970s, most neoconservatives had little, if any, political experience beyond launching broadsides in magazines like *Commentary*, *Partisan Review*, and the *Public Interest*. Their apostasies in the Democratic Party had been approvingly recorded by *National Review*, which declared that Harvard professor Nathan Glazer's 1971 essay in *Commentary* about intellectuals "says about the Jewish intellectual establishment in America what no non-Jew could say without being thought prejudiced."[30] But the neoconservatives needed a horse inside the Democratic Party to run for the presidency.

30. *National Review*.

Their candidate was Senator Henry M. Jackson. A domestic liberal, a staunch backer of Israel, a fierce critic of the United Nations, and, above all, a foe of détente with the Soviet Union, Jackson became the most prominent neoconservative politician.

Like other neoconservatives, Jackson was profoundly shaped by World War II. As the son of Scandinavian immigrants, he would ask, "Of what avail to Norway's people was all its clean air and pure water once Hitler's troops had set foot on Norwegian soil?" A visit to the Buchenwald concentration camp in April 1945, as part of a congressional delegation, helped instill a lifelong support for Israel. Jackson put together what would become an influential advisory group of neoconservatives, including his aides Richard Perle, Charles Horner, and Elliott Abrams, as well as Princeton University professor Bernard Lewis, strategist Albert Wohlstetter, and Russian historian Richard Pipes.

On the face of it, Kissinger, a supporter of the Vietnam War and a Jewish émigré, should have been exactly the type of person to appeal to Jackson and other neoconservatives. But as Kissinger recounted in his memoirs, "To my astonishment, I found myself in confrontation with a former ally in what became an increasingly tense relationship. What made the conflict both strange and painful was that I felt more comfortable with Jackson on most issues than with many newfound allies."[31] For neoconservatives, ranging from Jackson to Moynihan to Podhoretz, Kissinger became Exhibit A of what was wrong with American foreign policy.

The neoconservatives succeeded in derailing détente. Jackson pushed the linkage of freedom of emigration for Jews with most-favored-nation status for the Soviet Union and obstructed Kissinger's arms-control negotiations with the Soviet Union. Kissinger fumed, calling Perle "a little bastard" and "a son of Mensheviks who thinks

---

31. Henry A. Kissinger, *Years of Upheaval* (Boston: Little, Brown & Co., 1982), 250.

all Bolsheviks are evil." Nixon declared "that a storm will hit American Jews if they are intransigent." But the Republican Party was already moving to the Right. Kissinger recalled in his memoirs that Nixon, "great tactician that he was, never conceived that he, the renowned Cold Warrior, would in the end be attacked from his old base on the right wing of the Republican Party." But presidential candidate Ronald Reagan declared that "[u]nder Kissinger and Ford, this nation has become number two in a world where it is dangerous—if not fatal—to be second best."

Not until 1979 did the neoconservatives and Reagan join forces. James Nuechterlein, writing in the May 1996 *First Things*, noted that "few if any neoconservatives were early supporters of Reagan, whom they correctly viewed as a traditionalist conservative with strong libertarian leanings. Prior to 1980, most neoconservatives regarded him with a combination of condescension and mistrust."[32] It was the Carter era, with its insistence on continuing Kissinger's détente with the Soviet Union, that convinced Podhoretz and others that Reagan was the answer. The neoconservative vehicle in the 1970s was the Coalition for a Democratic Majority. It was created in the early 1970s by labor leaders and neoconservative intellectuals, who warned that Carter was succumbing to illusions about the Soviet threat. (This coalition still formally exists on paper.) In his essay *The Present Danger*, Podhoretz made the case for moralpolitik versus realpolitik, worrying that the Iranian hostage crisis and the Soviet invasion of Afghanistan represented "the final collapse of an American resolve to resist the forward surge of Soviet imperialism."[33]

It's easy enough to mock such apprehensions in retrospect, but at the time the Soviet Union did seem to be on the right side of history and the United States on the retreat. Reagan's arms buildup, the Strategic Defense Initiative, and depiction of the Soviet Union as

32. James Nuechterlein, *First Things* (May 1996): 14–15.
33. Norman Podhoretz, *The Present Danger* (New York: Simon and Schuster, 1980), 3.

an "evil empire," however, seemed to signal that the United States
was back on the offensive. Neoconservatives backed the administration to the hilt and seemed themselves to be on the winning side
once the Soviet imperium collapsed. So definitive did the victory
appear that Podhoretz, among others, began publishing requiems for
the neoconservative movement. Then, as Podhoretz astutely noted,
Bill Clinton, after a lackluster beginning, started to embrace neoconservative principles. He stared down the Serbs in Bosnia and Kosovo,
sent gunships off Haiti, and bombed Afghanistan and Sudan. Meanwhile, the GOP lashed out at Clinton, denouncing humanitarian
intervention and, indeed, seeming to return to isolationist principles,
at least in the House of Representatives, where Tom DeLay, among
others, decried the use of U.S. military power abroad. As Joshua
Muravchik pointed out, it was the realists in the GOP who wanted
to do nothing when hostilities first broke out in Bosnia: "then-Pres-
ident George H. W. Bush dismissed them as a 'hiccup,' while Secretary of State James Baker declared: 'We have no dog in that fight.'
These two were not heartless men, but they were exemplars of a
traditional conservative cast of mind. The essence of the matter, as
they saw it, was that Bosnia engaged little in the way of American
interests, which in the conventional view meant vital resources, or
strategic geography, or the safety of allies."[34] It was no coincidence
that Richard Perle and Paul Wolfowitz, among others, worked closely
with human rights organizations to rouse more support for the Bosnians as they faced the marauding Serbs, who were intent on a gen-
ocidal land grab (a stance, incidentally, that seems to have eluded
some opponents of the Iraq war, who dismiss Wolfowitz's concern
with the suppression of the Kurds and Shiittes by Saddam Hussein's
forces as so much window dressing).[35] With the Democrats pursuing

34. Joshua Muravchik, "The Neoconservative 'Cabal,'" *Commentary* (September
2003): 32.
35. Wolfowitz, for instance, made no secret of his unhappiness with the reluctance of the first Bush administration and, initially, the Clinton administration to

a more aggressive foreign policy, there was really no need for neo-conservatism any longer. Or was there?

The truth is that the current divide in the Republican Party—between those like George F. Will and those further on the fringes, such as Patrick Buchanan, who assail neoconservatives for big government nation-building in Iraq—was already present in the 1990s. It was Irving Kristol's son's attempt to create "national greatness conservatism" that is at the bottom of the rift in the Bush administration. In a 1996 *Foreign Affairs* article, William Kristol and Robert Kagan wrote "Toward a Neo-Reaganite Foreign Policy," which called for aggressively promoting democracy abroad. In the pages of *The Wall Street Journal* in 1997, Kristol and David Brooks elaborated on this theme. They urged conservatives to incorporate progressive American nationalists into the conservative pantheon—Alexander Hamilton, Henry Clay, and Teddy Roosevelt. "How can Americans love their nation if they hate its government?" asked Kristol and Brooks.[36]

The response from small-government traditionalists, led by writers from *National Review*'s orbit, was quick. "No aspect of our lives has escaped assault by government," economist Paul Craig Roberts declared. "The Constitution of the United States has been reduced to a scrap of paper."[37] The *National Review* itself complained, "Our usable past won't all fit into a be-happy Op-Ed piece."

Today, similar complaints are voiced by a growing chorus of traditional conservatives. Some argue that the influence of neoconser-

---

aid the Bosnians: "Of the many failures of Western policy in the former Yugoslavia, none was more important or more contemptible than the failure to provide the government of Bosnia with the means to defend itself from the campaign of 'ethnic cleansing' launched by Milosevic, the ruler of Serbia, and his Bosnian Serb henchmen led by Kardzic and Mladic." Paul Wolfowitz, "The Man Who Saved the Day—Sort of . . . ," *National Interest* (Fall 1998): 102.

36. William Kristol and David Brooks, "What Ails Conservatism," *Wall Street Journal,* 15 September 1997: A16

37. Paul Craig Roberts, "Government and the Country," *Washington Times*, 19 September 1997.

vatism has been grossly exaggerated. They even come close to writing it out of existence. "Long before the neoconservatives came along," contended Ramesh Ponnuru, "Barry Goldwater saw that the Soviet Union's foreign policy was not a mere extension of traditional Russian imperialism but was inseparable from its Communist ideology and practice."[38] Others yearn for the days when Senator Robert Taft, a leading light of the party in the 1940s and 1950s known as "Mr. Republican," decried America's entry into NATO and its sponsorship of the Marshall Plan to rebuild Europe: "No foreign policy can be justified except a policy devoted . . . to the protection of the liberty of the American people, with war only as the last resort and only to protect that liberty." But as more sensible Republicans, such as William F. Buckley Jr., recognized, "In order to fight communism, we may have to accept bureaucratic totalitarianism on these shores" because communism was "the greatest danger the West has ever faced."

With the end of the cold war and despite September 11, the difficulties of the Iraq war continue to stir doubts. Is it not possible that the Iraq venture, so muddled in execution, was fated for failure? A May 3 *National Review* editorial, called "An End to Illusion," lamented "an underestimation in general of the difficulty of implanting democracy in alien soil, and an overestimation in particular of the sophistication of what is fundamentally still a tribal society. And one devastated by decades of tyranny." But it politely states that "Iraq was not a Wilsonian—or a 'neoconservative'—war. It was broadly supported by the Right as a war of national interest."[39]

Well, maybe. But as William Kristol recently remarked in the *New York Times*, "If we have to make common cause with the more hawkish liberals and fight the conservatives, that is fine with me." This suggests that neoconservatism's political peregrinations may not

38. Ramesh Ponnuru, "Getting to the Bottom of This 'Neo' Nonsense," *National Review* (June 16, 2003): 30.
39. "An End to Illusion," *National Review* (May 3, 2004): 14, 16.

be over.[40] The truth is that Iraq was a neoconservative war in its optimism about remaking Iraq and implanting liberal democracy in the Middle East. The project to transform the Middle East would have been unthinkable without being championed by such senior officials as Wolfowitz. After September 11, the defection to neoconservative ideas, if not to the movement itself, by former Trotskyists such as Christopher Hitchens and Paul Berman suggests how powerful the belief in confronting offensively, not defensively, Islamic totalitarian movements has become, and remains, despite the impasse in Iraq.

Until now, President Bush has largely endorsed the neoconservative program in the Middle East. It is not too much to say that Bush is a neoconservative, someone who Wolfowitz said during the 2000 campaign reminded him of "Scoop" Jackson. In a new version of dictatorships and double standards, Bush maintains that it is racist to believe that Arabs are unfit for democracy. Far from being a passive conduit for a neoconservative cabal, Bush believes wholeheartedly in upending the Middle East. Indeed, if neoconservative officials in the administration are right, Bush himself has been pushing the pace against a reluctant bureaucracy. Unlike Reagan, who was reluctant to intervene militarily abroad and relied on proxies, Bush has aggressively prosecuted the war on terrorism.

If the administration fails in Iraq, many conservatives will endorse a kind of realpolitik that has not served the GOP well in the past. Neoconservatives won't. It would be no small irony if the neoconservatives once again become a small faction, as they were in the early 1970s, uncomfortable in either the Republican or Democratic Parties. In a reversal of their long-standing intellectual role, they might even find themselves disputing more with conservatives than liberals in coming years.

In the *National Review*, at the height of neoconservative influence

---

40. David D. Kirkpatrick, "Lack of Resolution in Iraq Finds Conservatives Divided," *New York Times*, 19 April 2004: A21.

in April 2003, David Frum ended a lengthy attack on paleoconservatives by declaring that unpatriotic conservatives "have turned their backs on their country. Now we turn our backs on them."[41] But the reverse may occur as the GOP descends into a fight between realists and neoconservatives that could prove as poisonous to the Republicans as were the foreign policy fights that racked the Democratic Party during the 1970s and 1980s. Just as Democrats shied away from an activist foreign policy for decades following Vietnam, so too a Bush defeat in November could trigger a prolonged civil war inside the GOP over the use of U.S. power at home and abroad.

But if Bush wins re-election, the opposite will occur. Contrary to myth, Bush has not been hijacked by neoconservatives. Instead, he is, if anything, an even more ardent proponent of intervention than many of his advisors. Consider his June 2, 2004, speech to the Air Force Academy, in which he depicted himself as Reagan's legatee. In a passage that has not received the attention it deserves, Bush declared, "[A]s events in Europe determined the outcome of the Cold War, events in the Middle East will set the course of our current struggle. If that region is abandoned to dictators and terrorists, it will be a constant source of violence and alarm, exporting killers of increasing destructive power to attack America and other free nations. If that region grows in democracy and prosperity and hope, the terrorist movement will lose its sponsors, lose its recruits, and lose the festering grievances that keep terrorists in business. The stakes of this struggle are high. The security and peace of our country are at stake, and success in this struggle is our only option."[42]

If Bush wins re-election and the GOP retains its Senate majority, neoconservatives will likely remain influential. The main targets in a Bush second term would be Syria and Iran. Already Bush has imposed

41. David Frum, "Unpatriotic Conservatives," *National Review* (April 7, 2003): 40.

42. "President Bush Speaks at Air Force Academy Graduation," www .whitehouse.gov/news/releases/2004/06/20040602.html.

sanctions against Syria. Nor would neoconservatism vanish if Bush loses. As Senators Joseph I. Lieberman and Jon Kyl's recent reconstitution of the Committee on Present Danger indicates, the movement is not going away; rather, it is preparing to revive itself as a kind of counterestablishment that criticizes both Democrats and Republicans for failing to face up to the dangers posed by militant Islam. It is perhaps as critics, rather than as policy makers, that neoconservatives will be most effective. As Irving Kristol, the godfather of the neoconservatives, wrote in the *Weekly Standard*, neoconservatism is "enjoying a second life" under Bush. Foes on the Right and Left may be eager to bury, not praise, the neoconservatives, but the obsequies are entirely premature.

CHAPTER SIX

Neoconservatism's Liberal Legacy

Tod Lindberg

"NEOCONSERVATISM" IS THE NAME of a robust strain in American intellectual life and American politics, a strain with a very rich history. But although even some of its leading figures over the years have pronounced the end of neoconservatism and therefore, presumably, the end of "the neoconservatives," usually on grounds of its and their merger with (or perhaps takeover of) the conservative mainstream, the term remains very much alive. This is especially true when used to describe a certain group of people who have sought to influence American public policy, most notably foreign policy in the post–cold war era, and who, in the administration of George W. Bush, obtained that influence.

One might, therefore, begin a consideration of neoconservatism with its rich history—or, in the alternative, with its contemporary influence. I propose to do neither (though I will indeed touch upon the past and the present). Instead, I explore here its future—specifically, the ways in which neoconservatism has evolved according to its own premises in the direction of a current and future politics dedicated to the preservation and extension of liberal order, properly understood. To get to neoconservatism's liberal legacy, however, it is necessary to begin with liberalism's origins in the nature of politics itself.

A Short Derivation of Liberalism

No single political view ever amounts to the *totality* of politics. Politics is, in a fundamental sense, about the management of difference and disagreement. If everyone shared the same interests, or thought exactly the same thing about all subjects of any importance, politics would be *unnecessary* (indeed, impossible). Short of that, if everyone agreed on a method for resolving all disputes that might arise between any given two people, politics would be *completed*, in the sense that relations between any given two people would either be correct (agreement) or would be subject to mutually accepted juridical mechanisms (in short, agreement over what to do about disagreement).[1]

We have certainly seen instances in which governments have sought to expunge disagreement from politics: this is the history of totalitarianism in the twentieth century. Stripped of its police powers, this totalitarianism is nothing other than the insistence that there is *one* correct answer to *all* relevant questions, that it is known to the state, and that no other answer is legitimate. But, of course, it makes no sense to speak of totalitarianism stripped of its police powers, because in the absence of agreement, the only way to promote uniformity of view is through repression. In fact, a politics of repression, while denying the existence of disagreement, actually presupposes disagreement, otherwise no repression would be necessary.

In the United States—though, of course, not only in the United States—disagreement manifests itself most broadly in the rejection of one or the other or both of the two major political parties. But political disagreement can hardly be said to end there. Within each major

1. For a rigorous analysis of juridical relations, see Alexandre Kojève, *Outline of a Phenomenology of Right*, trans. Bryan-Paul Frost and Robert Howse (Lanham, MD: Rowman and Littlefield, 2000).

political party, there are, broadly speaking, two wings, which reflect internal disagreement about the direction the party should take. Within each of the wings, some consider themselves harder-line and some consider themselves more moderate. Indeed, for every "on the one hand," there is an "on the other hand," all the way down to any given two people—which is to say, any given two people are different. (Even people who are in agreement agree about *something*: they agree in relation to some thing or things but not in relation to all things. The two people are not the same, and they understand each other to differ from one another. However much you and I agree, if I am hungry, it is a matter of consequence to me whether I myself eat or you do. We cannot agree that I am you and you are me.)

It is therefore not difficult to see that politics is constituted by the interaction of various contending points of view—that is, disagreement—and the resolution of this disagreement in the here and now. Political history is a record of the interaction and working out of the disagreements of the moment, whether this management of disagreement takes the form of world war, revolution, the convening of a council of elders, an election, a vote in parliament, arbitration, or the drawing of straws.

I would venture to say that in a reasonably well-ordered democratic polity, which I take the United States to be, the major poles of disagreement, in this case the Democratic and Republican Parties, tend to balance one another over time, making adjustments in relation to what they stand for in order to broaden their appeal to voters. And we are better off with a politics in which Democrats and Republicans contend than we would be if either one or the other won "once and for all." In fact, one could look at the evolution of the positions of the two parties over time as a continuous rebalancing, helping to ensure that no permanent victor emerges. Of course, this is not what the politicians see themselves as doing: they are looking for votes. Some hard-line partisans—those who entertain the view that all members of the other party are either wicked or stupid or ignorant or deluded or in some other fashion entirely wrong—entertain fantasies about total victory, the final vanquishing of the other party. But just the same, the way in which they look for votes seems to have the effect of creating a continuous rebalancing. The specific strength of this liberal democratic politics in the context of procuring agreement is that (rhetorical heat notwithstanding) each party feels vested in the system, even in the face of defeat, because of the hope and expectation of eventual victory. Politicians may be looking to win "once and for all," but the losing party at the polls in any given election will never declare it has been defeated "once and for all." On the contrary, loser and winner both look to the next election.

Although neither party may reasonably expect victory "once and for all," in the United States there are, in fact, many formerly political questions that appear to have been resolved "once and for all" by the emergence of complete agreement. For example, slavery is no longer a political question because no one proposes to bring it back. Even those who insist that Aristotle and Nietzsche be given their due in full do not suggest that these philosophers' analyses of the rank order of human souls require latter-day advocacy of slavery so that the slavish can be the slaves they should be. Other matters of complete agreement include the following propositions: States may not secede from the Union. Women have equal rights in the workplace. Dueling is not an acceptable means to settle disputes. Parental rights over children are limited in that parents may not, for example, dispose of unwanted female infants. The change from a $20 bill I receive in Washington, D.C., I can spend in Palo Alto, California.[2] These "once and for all" issues are usually codified as matters of law or right, but they are also firmly entrenched as social practice quite apart from their legal status. It would not occur to an aspiring politician to make his central issue the desirability of his state's secession from the United

2. The complicated web of relations embodied in the use of paper money is one of John R. Searle's main examples in *The Construction of Social Reality* (New York: Free Press, 1997).

States. He would be dismissed as a crackpot.[3] The proof of this is the absence, for more than a century, of any such character in American politics.

It is not enough to argue that politics is driven by human difference and has as its task the management of the disagreement ensuing from difference; that a politics of repression, however brutal, cannot hope in the end to overcome difference by imposing agreement; and that the only hope for a successful politics is one that creates the conditions in which people can accept and respect difference, each with regard to the other—which is to say, respect each other's freedom. In addition, one must observe that a person desires not merely freedom for the moment but rather lasting freedom. Unless such a person is prepared to try to secure his or her freedom by force, the only way to secure it is through mutual recognition of the freedom of another, notwithstanding the *difference* of the other—in other words, recognition of the *freedom and equality* of the other. A person recognizes the freedom and equality of the other as the condition of the other's recognition of his or her freedom and equality. The mutual recognition of each as free and equal I take to be the *constitutive* characteristic of liberalism.

Yet freedom and equality do not necessarily go together. To pick an extreme example, a tyrant may be free in that he has the power to compel others to do what he wishes, whereas no one else has the power to compel him to act against his own wishes. One can also imagine (in fact, one can turn to history rather than the imagination) an equality that seeks to obliterate all difference manifesting itself as freedom. In a liberal society, however, *liberal politics* is a matter of balancing the competing claims of the desire for freedom and the

3. He would be dismissed not so much because of his view as because of his insistence on taking his view to the public square, that is, on making it a political issue. Princeton University's Peter Singer, for example, famously made the case for a right to infanticide. But he never ran for public office on that platform, preferring instead to advocate his views from the position of his chair in bioethics.

desire for equality. The highest good of liberal society is neither simply freedom nor simply equality but the blend of the two as freedom *and* equality. The balance one seeks is "as much freedom as is consistent with equality," where equality is understood to be the mutual recognition of freedom.

But what about demands for freedom that might impinge upon the equality of all? Or demands made in the name of equality that may impinge upon freedom? These are precisely the dangers that inhere in liberal politics. They amount to the risk that liberal society contains within it the seeds of its own destruction. Even if this were true of a particular liberal society, it would not affect my judgment that liberalism counts as the final answer in politics—mutual recognition of the freedom and equality of each as the highest possible human political achievement. By "possible," I mean that there is no obstacle, in principle, to universal liberalism in this sense becoming actual. But what is true of liberal*ism* is not necessarily true of any given liberal society or state. There is, unfortunately, no available guarantee that the advantageous balance of disagreement that liberalism generally manages to strike will hold in all cases.[4]

People may press for freedoms that are inconsistent with the claims of equality, essentially by seeking recognition for the special claims of those who are unwilling to grant recognition of the equality of others in return. In this way, a liberal society risks empowering the illiberal—those who would take advantage of the benefits available in a society of free and equal persons who mutually recognize their freedom and equality by using that freedom for the purpose of pressing their *exclusive* (i.e., anti-egalitarian) claims upon that society.

Likewise, people in a liberal society may make demands pertaining to equality that impinge excessively upon the freedom of individuals. I have been describing equality in formal terms: mutual recognition.

4. A chilling account of the breakdown of liberal order is available in Howard M. Sachar, *Dreamland: Europeans and Jews in the Aftermath of the Great War* (New York: Knopf, 2002).

But it is clear that equality has content as well. As to the precise nature of that content, I am not prepared to state a case here, for reasons to which I shall return. I do not think, however, that we will find the answer through recourse to a Rawlsian "original position,"[5] which I would characterize as a noble attempt to squeeze from politics its very essence—namely, difference and the disagreement that attends it. Nor do I think we will find the answer in the opposite insistence that equality remain merely formal and that no social claims against individuals be allowed in the name of equality, as, for example, Robert Nozick would argue.[6] The truth lies somewhere between, in the strong sense that *all* extant liberal societies do in fact strike a balance between freedom and equality. One might add that states *differ* in where they strike it while still retaining an essentially liberal character. It is also worth noting that states *restrike* it and restrike it again over time.

Is this ongoing rebalancing directional in character? Does it point to an end? I think the evidence suggests it does. Again, this evidence takes the form of the seemingly permanent disappearance of disagreement about certain things that used to be contentious. We have discussed the disappearance of disagreement over slavery. It seems unlikely to me that anyone in a liberal society (more precisely, any liberal in a liberal society, which is to say, a society in which the illiberal are absent or marginalized) will ever try to take away women's right to vote. There will be no movement for a constitutional amendment overturning the Supreme Court and imposing a ban on sodomy. But note again that the directionality is neither simply toward more and more freedom nor simply toward more and more equality. I do not think there will come a time when expanding demands for freedom produce the return of smoking on airplanes. Although each of

5. John Rawls, *A Theory of Justice* (Cambridge, MA: Belknap/Harvard, 1971), 118–83.

6. "The minimal state is the most extensive state that can be justified. Any state more extensive violates people's rights." Robert Nozick, *Anarchy, State and Utopia* (New York: Basic Books, 1977), 149.

these two desires is present in liberal societies, once again, it is the balance between the two that matters, that moves, and that defines a direction.

One could say that one favors individual freedom as long as it does not impinge on the freedom of others, but this has the unfortunate effect of bringing the discussion to a halt at precisely the point at which it becomes interesting because it is difficult. It seems to me that what is emerging is a balance between socially validated (i.e., mutually recognized and mutually practiced) individual rights and individual responsibilities. The endpoint would accordingly be a condition in which, as a matter of everyday practice, people acted in accordance with their responsibilities in the expectation that others would act in accordance with their responsibilities. "Rights" as things in need of protection would disappear, as would "politics" in the sense used here—namely, as the management of disagreement—because disagreement would give way to agreement (including agreement to disagree and mutually agreed juridical mechanisms for the resolution of remaining disputes).[7]

I have offered here a formal account of the endpoint. I cannot give the content of the endpoint (though it is interesting to speculate). I am not, however, obliged to try to do so, because an adequate formal account is sufficient. As a matter of social practice, however, until we reach the endpoint,[8] there will be cases in which the demand for

7. I grant that this endpoint presupposes a world in which a person's responsibilities are nonconflicting. The point is that I am giving an account of how such a world comes about—in essence, how we get to agreement about what constitutes an impermissible infringement on someone else's freedom.

8. The question of how we know we have reached the endpoint is interesting. The epistemological problem is that the reappearance of disagreement is proof that we have not, but the continuation of agreement is not proof that we have. As a practical matter, it strikes me that it will become harder and harder to deny that the endpoint has been achieved. Another way to put this is that phenomenologically, the "endpoint" can only be perceived as something one is approaching asymptotically: One knows what it is but not when one has arrived at it, even though the suspicion that one has indeed arrived grows and grows. The final state of political

equality will indeed impinge excessively on freedom, just as in other cases the demand for freedom will impinge on equality.

We arrive, therefore, at our politics of the future: because we favor freedom and equality, and as a consequence of our general support for efforts to extend freedom and equality, we must also oppose such demands for equality that impinge excessively on freedom and oppose such demands for freedom that impinge excessively on equality.

Whether one wishes to call this position "neoconservative" or something else, it is both "neo" and "conservative" in the sense that what is being conserved is our liberalism—its extension in time and space. The distinction between this "neoconservative" position and a "progressive" position amounts to the weight one attaches to two sets of claims. One set, the "progressive," manifests itself as the demand for expanded freedom *or* the demand for greater substantive equality in the particular case at hand (that is, in the object of a political dispute). The other set, "neoconservative," concerns itself with whether a demand for greater freedom might impinge excessively on substantive equality or whether a demand for greater substantive equality might impinge excessively on freedom. If neoconservatism has a claim for the superiority of its outlook, it is that the desire for freedom and the desire for equality are always present in liberal societies and liberal politics (indeed, they are the raw material of liberal society), whereas the striking of an acceptable balance between the two is not a given but a matter to be worked out by politics—a politics that can go badly wrong when the balance is wrongly struck, potentially with disastrously illiberal consequences.

---

dialogue, which is to say the articulation of difference, will accordingly be between those who think the end has arrived and those who think one cannot say. This should allay all concern that the future will be boring, because this dialogue is nothing other than the continuation of the debate over the possibility of absolute wisdom. This is a debate we have been having since Hegel claimed to possess such wisdom. Hegel is doing very well in this debate, with little help from his friends— far better than he seemed to be doing in the nineteenth and twentieth centuries. In any case, the debate has not been boring.

The Turn to "Reality"

Any reading of the intellectual history of the tendency known as "neo-conservatism" will quickly reveal that its leading figures cannot fairly be said to have seen matters in the light I am describing. At the same time, it is quite possible to see in their thinking many of the seeds of our current and future politics, the conservation of liberalism. I don't intend to offer anything like a systematic or comprehensive survey. I rather sketch the ways in which certain ideas propagated mainly by a loose group of New York intellectuals prove antecedent to what I am describing here.

It is not at all difficult to see that neoconservatism, as it emerged in the 1960s, was first of all a response to postwar American political liberalism, a sufficiently widely held secular faith as to constitute almost a consensus politics. An essential characteristic of that political liberalism was its faith that government intervention on a sufficiently large scale could solve, or at least ameliorate, the effects of the social problems of the day, especially poverty and racial discrimination. Postwar political liberalism also had an international component, including the assertive use of American power in the containment of the Soviet Union and, more generally, in defense of a liberal and liberalizing "free world." (This picture would become more compli-cated, of course, with Vietnam and the emergence of a left-wing American politics sharply critical of American power abroad and the justice of the American regime at home.)

Now, this postwar political liberalism has only a tenuous connec-tion to liberalism in the broader sense in which I am using the term; but there is a connection nonetheless. The raw material of liberalism, the fraternal desires for freedom and equality, are intrinsically expan-sionist in character and point to a limit—namely, the claim that free-dom and equality are universal goods.[9] To the extent that the political

9. If a balanced freedom and equality constitute the highest good in politics—

liberals of the postwar era made sweeping claims about universals, they were speaking the language of liberalism in its classical or broader sense. Thus, in a sense, neoconservatism began as a dialogue with liberalism and, in fact, emerged out of it—something old-style conservatives would never say of themselves.[10] In fact, once radical politics supplanted or transformed the meaning of postwar liberalism for the Left, a common refrain among the neoconservatives was that they had not changed, but liberalism had.

In Irving Kristol's famous definition, a neoconservative is "a liberal who has been mugged by reality." This is to say, certain stubborn facts about the world did violence to the optimistic aspirations of postwar political liberalism. This point is important for two reasons: First, it places the here and now front and center. Upon the (in principle) universal aspirations of liberalism and upon the current goals of liberal public policy, reality impinges, sometimes decisively.

---

the final answer, as I have claimed—then there is no basis for a claim that one human being should be treated as an equal but another one should not, or that one is entitled to freedom but the other is not, except in cases where the other's desire for freedom is unaccompanied by a desire for equality, or vice versa.

10. As to whether the old-style conservatives are correct, that is a different matter. Harvey Mansfield distinguished "the modern conservatism that accompanies liberalism from the classical conservatism that preceded liberalism," arguing that the modern sort of conservative, "unlike Burke, does not know what he shares with liberalism." Harvey C. Mansfield Jr., *The Spirit of Liberalism* (Cambridge, MA: Harvard University Press, 1978), x. I would think that a serious challenge to liberalism would have to involve a repudiation of its constitutive characteristics, namely, the desires for freedom and equality and the directionality toward a limit condition of universality thereby implied. That repudiation, in turn, would seem to me to entail a defense of inequality and of freedom only for the highest type, as well as an according rejection of any extension of the privileges earned by the strengths of the highest beyond their ranks. Nietzsche attempted this as philosophy, and the Nazis as politics. But what connection these efforts have with anything in contemporary conservatism is hard to see. In William F. Buckley Jr.'s adage that a conservative stands athwart history shouting "stop," there would not seem to be much expectation of success in stopping history. It is more an articulation of an attitude toward acquiescence. And even my formal description here of what a repudiation of liberalism might entail does not escape the horizon of liberalism itself but rather takes its shape from an understanding of the character of liberalism.

The getting from here to there is not a matter simply of will or declaration; rather, it entails resistance of a kind both foreseeable and unforeseeable. A policy that purports to compel a certain behavior en route to a certain outcome may or may not so compel the behavior and achieve the desired outcome. And in accordance with the law of unintended consequences, the most consequential outcomes may be far different from those the policy makers sought. A jobs training program (to pick one policy area out of multitudes discussed, especially in the pages of the *Public Interest*) does not necessarily result in (1) an individual trained to do a job and, further, (2) employment for the individual trained.

It is hard to overstate the importance of this turn—the neoconservative turn—in thinking about public policy. It is often described as a preference for "empirical" tests of policy outcomes. The juxtaposition is as against, on one hand, the naïve assumption that intention equals result (jobs training is "good" because people lack the skills they need to get jobs, and training will give them those skills) and, on the other, objections to policy proposals based solely on first principles. Jobs training cannot "work" because of the intrinsic incompetence of government; jobs training is no business of government in any case; innovation in policy will, in all likelihood (if not in all cases), make matters worse. Instead of settling policy matters by having ideologues argue over principle—and it is probably no accident that conservatives were losing those arguments—social scientists would step in to investigate whether social programs were delivering on the promises advocates made on their behalf and would test for other, perhaps unanticipated, effects.

This description of neoconservativism was, and is, popular among those who identify themselves as neoconservatives,[11] and it is true as far as it goes. But a critical engagement with it is also necessary. Soon

11. See, for example, Adam Wolfson, "Conservatives and Neoconservatives," *Public Interest* 154 (Spring 2003).

enough, the weight of empirical evidence led to *neoconservative* generalizations—which is to say, cases in principle—about which social policy approaches would or would not work. Such generalizations were inevitable insofar as questions about whether to adopt a particular public policy were politically salient: one could be neutral, but the proposition that only after adopting a policy can one properly evaluate it is indistinguishable from acquiescence in its adoption. Neoconservatives believed they had good reason to oppose certain kinds of policy proposals based on previous empirical experience. What began (in some cases) as an attempt to get past ideology (liberal or conservative) through empirical tests of "what works" became ideological in its own right, as neoconservatives, no less than others, took positions based on (empirically derived, or at least empirically justified) principle. Although the result may have been richer and more sophisticated analysis and argument, any notion that empirical approaches could altogether displace preference based on principles was mistaken.

And what was this emergent preference? I think it is not unfair to describe the neoconservative conclusion as follows: Reality is such that efforts to alter it result in its mugging you—often enough, that is, to render such efforts dubious at best. One should reduce one's ambitions accordingly.

The essential contribution of the neoconservative turn was to introduce reality (how things are) as a counterweight to aspiration (what you want)—in this case, postwar liberal aspiration. This turn was an extraordinary achievement and produced profound effects, most notably, a scaling back on unreasonable expectations about the state's ability to impose social change. But it was incomplete. Here, "reality" was presented as something unchanging and rigid. But do we really want to say that of reality? Certainly, the past is fixed, has shaped the present, and weighs heavily on the future. And the *idea* of reality is unchanging. But the *reality* of reality—which is to say its content, unfolding in the here and now—does change. This opens up possibilities: if *what you want* (a change) is in accordance with *how things are*, then you can have your change. Reality not only resists but also enables change. The task, then, becomes the examination of the content of reality to determine which attempts to change it would be in accordance with it—that is, inhere in it—and which attempted changes would run counter to it (and be mugged by it).[12]

I submit that we have now arrived at (or returned to) the political task of our liberalism, namely, balancing the desire for freedom and the desire for equality. The proper response to a mugging by reality is not the abandonment of liberalism, broadly construed, in favor of a preliberal or antiliberal or "conservative" alternative, neo- or otherwise, but rather the abandonment of those elements (rife in postwar liberalism) that reality would not accommodate in favor of those that reality would accommodate and, indeed, compel. This is our current and future politics.

The Resilience of the Liberal Economic Order

From its early years, neoconservativism was engaged across the full range of public policy matters, domestic (especially in the *Public Interest*) and foreign (especially in *Commentary*). There were self-identified neoconservative scholars of welfare and education and housing and crime policy, of Latin America and arms control and the Soviet Union. But any serious review of the main currents of the substance of neoconservative thought (as opposed to its "empirical" methodology, discussed above) would have no difficulty quickly identifying two central and related themes: the neoconservative critique of capitalism

---

12. One could say this in a more technical fashion by adopting Hegel's terminology: The Concept is in accord with itself. There is unity of essence (what is) and existence (that is). Needless to say, this has been a matter of some philosophical controversy in the years since. One could, with some justice, characterize the history of philosophy since Hegel as a series of confrontations with this proposition.

and the neoconservative revitalization of anticommunism during the cold war.

The neoconservative critique of capitalism[13] drew heavily on Max Weber's *The Protestant Ethic and the Spirit of Capitalism*. In the neo-conservative view, capitalism—salutary though it was with respect to the efficient allocation of goods and services and accordingly unpar-alleled as a means for the advancement of people's material prosper-ity—was in crisis. The source of this crisis was the deficiency of self-propulsion of capitalism itself. Capitalism, in this view, required something neither contained within nor perpetuated by its system of market economics. This "something" was, in effect, Weber's Protes-tant ethic: a set of virtues or habits of character—including thrift, industry, temperance, patience, persistence, and so forth—whose ori-gin and sustenance came from religious faith and the expectation of salvation as a reward for right earthly conduct. In the absence of these virtues, capitalism could not flourish. Yet capitalism itself did nothing to encourage the virtues upon which it depended. On the contrary, in certain respects, capitalist consumer society worked to undermine those virtues. Whereas once Americans thought it morally praisewor-thy and necessary to save money for future consumption, with the arrival of installment credit in the early twentieth century, the habit of deferred gratification gave way to a demand for instant gratification. In the long run, the demand for instant gratification would subvert properly functioning markets and the long-term time horizon required for the success of capitalism.

The neoconservative critique of capitalism did not see its contra-dictions resulting in a proletarian revolution, ushering in a new stage of history. But neither did it counter Marxist claims to that effect with the simple pronouncement that the market was all right. Capi-

13. For the definitive articulation of the neoconservative critique of capitalism, see Daniel Bell, *The Cultural Contradictions of Capitalism* (New York: Basic Books, 1978), and the essays collected in Irving Kristol, *Two Cheers for Capitalism* (New York: Basic Books, 1978).

talism, in the neoconservative view, was indeed problematic. As to
what might follow from its further collapse under the weight of its
cultural contradictions, the neoconservative critique offered no certain
vision beyond a general portrait of decadence and stagnation. There
was also an essential ambiguity in the neoconservative critique over
the inevitability of capitalism's decline. On one hand, the conclusion
that follows from the premise of the argument would seem to be that
decline is inevitable. On the other, there was the possibility that capitalism might find renewed spirit (at least for a time) through the
cultivation or recultivation of precisely those Protestant virtues that
marked its rise.

So it was that the theorizing yielded a political agenda, namely,
the need for a robust defense of ordinary, bourgeois life. As a type,
the bourgeois has been under attack for centuries—starting with
Rousseau, who identified the species as a timid and diminished
human type; later, and perhaps most famously, by Marx as the tool
and dupe of a capitalist economic order that in turn would fall to
proletarian revolution, taking the bourgeoisie down with it. Most
recently, an assault on bourgeois life was at the heart of the emergence
of the 1960s counterculture and the beginning of its institutionali-
zation in the 1970s.

But, the neoconservatives asked, was this bourgeois fellow really
so bad, so base as all that? Was he not, in fact, the living repository
of the "values" or virtues that enabled the capitalist system to persist?
And were those values not, upon closer examination, morally preferable on their own terms to the relativism and even nihilism often
embraced by his critics? Were the critics not, in certain respects, the
material beneficiaries of the very values for which they had such contempt? And was our bourgeois not, therefore, worth defending against
a pitiless cultural assault on the moral legitimacy of his very existence?
And if, in turn, the bourgeois type could be defended in such a
fashion as to allow for the "moral capital" of capitalism to remain
sufficient for the operation of the system, then it became possible to

envision a future for capitalism that was not quite so gloomy. This was all the more so if there were specific policy measures one might identify as contributing to the decline of moral capital—for example, those encouraging able-bodied people to rely on the state for sustenance. With the reversal of these poor policy choices, one might envision a certain amount of "remoralization," though, again, it is rather difficult to say whether the neoconservative critique as a theoretical proposition could allow for anything but eventual decline.

As it happened, by the mid-1980s, many of those traveling under the "neoconservative" label (whether they did so voluntarily or not) had abandoned the original neoconservative critique of capitalism. There were, no doubt, many reasons for abandoning it, including the abatement of inflation and the beginning of a long period of economic growth following the 1982 recession. Stagnation and decline no longer looked to be quite so certain an eventual future as they did in the 1970s. Moreover, with the arrival of glasnost and perestroika in Mikhail Gorbachev's Soviet Union, centrally planned economies no longer looked to be at all a viable alternative to, even if a poorer performer than, market economies. It became increasingly clear that central planning was a route to economic disaster. The notion that a centrally planned system was somehow going to displace the market systems that were doing so well became less and less plausible.

I think, however, that the most important reason for the neoconservative abandonment of the neoconservative critique of capitalism is that it became harder and harder to find evidence regarding the "depleting moral capital" of capitalism. I do not mean by this that capitalism came somehow to be regarded as a source of moral regeneration or of morality (though some were willing to go that far); I only mean that the system's potential for self-perpetuation became more evident. In practice, the system did not lack, but rather seemed to embody, whatever "ethic" was necessary to propel market economies. This "ethic," moreover, was looking less and less Protestant in character and more and more entrepreneurial, involving the acceptance of risk in exchange for the prospect of reward.[14]

I take this view of the resilience of capitalism and market economics to be conventional wisdom now—and, moreover, to be correct. There is no longer any serious expectation of proletarian revolution, nor even of a widespread return, for political reasons, to the poor policy choices underlying centrally planned economies. "Globalization," which I take to be the uneven spread across the globe of capitalist accumulation of surplus, continues to press against the resistance of local custom and generally to prevail over it or to devise a local compromise. Antiglobalization protests are often incoherent, expressing numerous demands that the capitalist system itself would be in the best position to satisfy. For a truly alternative vision of how the world should be ordered, one must look to the likes of Osama bin Laden, and then one must ask how likely it is that his vision will prevail.

The historical importance of the neoconservative critique of capitalism was, I think, as an intellectual way station for sensible minds looking critically at the world around them and seeing, against the weight of all regnant theory, that capitalism or market economics worked rather well indeed. Perhaps the system is eventually doomed to collapse under the weight of its cultural contradictions—but not necessarily *soon*, and not beyond the ability of sound public policy to effect a delay. The sensible mind having been opened to the possibility that the system was not so quickly destined for the ash heap of history, it was thereby opened to the possibility that the system was not destined for the ash heap of history at all.

Once again, another real strength emerging here is the reconnection of capitalism to the real world: Rather than viewing the question of the future of capitalism in terms of dialectical materialism—or

14. I reviewed the neoconservative critique of capitalism at greater length in Tod Lindberg, "Four Cheers for Capitalism," *Commentary* 79, no. 4 (April 1985), in which I also laid out the objection to the Weberian perspective discussed here.

perhaps the minority alternative, of capitalism as a "natural" phenomenon except when undone by poor policy choices, or "government" more broadly—we begin to see a serious inquiry into what sort of creatures these participants in market economies really are. We see here a political dimension to the economic question. It will come as no great surprise that the content of that social dimension is our liberalism, the balancing of freedom and equality that the marketplace presupposes.

Extending the Liberal Space

The demise of Soviet communism substantially validated the triumph (if not the triumphalism) of capitalism. But though we can say that the revitalized anticommunism of neoconservatism abetted in the fall of the Berlin Wall, the breakup of the Warsaw Pact, and the disintegration of the Soviet Union itself, we must also note that neoconservatism never predicted those outcomes. At best, I think, neoconservatives pinned their hopes on the continued success and prosperity of the free world, the containment of Communist expansion, and perhaps the hope that the territory of the free world might expand; in any case, the Brezhnev Doctrine—that once a country became Communist, it would remain so—had to be rejected in principle and resisted where practical. But this never amounted to a hope, let alone an expectation, that capitalism was on the brink of worldwide triumph.

One defining characteristic of neoconservative anticommunism was its moralism,[15] which had two components. The first was a conviction, again running contrary to prevailing intellectual trends, that

15. The central figure in the neoconservative revitalization of anticommunism is Norman Podhoretz, both in his own writings and as editor of *Commentary*. See, for example, Norman Podhoretz, *The Present Danger* (New York: Simon and Schuster, 1980). For an explicitly moral critique of the realpolitik approach as exemplified by Henry Kissinger, see Norman Podhoretz, "Kissinger Reconsidered," *Commentary* 73, no. 6 (June 1982).

democratic government of the sort practiced in the United States was
worth defending on grounds of its moral superiority to competing
models. Democracy, contra Winston Churchill, was not the worst
form of government except for all the others; instead, it actually
reflected and protected the human desire for freedom or liberty in a
way that deserved recognition as "good." Concomitant with this view,
though by no means a necessary corollary of it and perhaps, if anything, even more contrary to prevailing intellectual opinion, was the
conviction that American power had, by and large, been a force for
good in the world, remained so, and ought to be increased to confront
the Soviet threat.

The second component was the conviction that communism was
singularly evil and, indeed, in the world of the cold war, uniquely
evil. Of course, the idea that communism was morally odious was
hardly a neoconservative invention. "Godless communism" had been
a staple of the rhetoric of the 1950s. The neoconservative moral vision
was both secular and more thoroughly grounded in political theory.[16]
Communism was a form of totalitarianism, the assertion by the state
of control over all aspects of people's lives. Traditional authoritarian
regimes, so the neoconservative argument ran, punished political dissent severely but often left open spheres of activity—for example,
economic life and family life—in which people were able to act relatively freely. Totalitarian states sought to obliterate these spheres of
freedom in the interest of greater control over their subjects' lives.

It was thus possible to assert a rank order among regime type:
democracy, good; authoritarian, ranging from benevolent to brutal
dictatorship, not good to bad; totalitarian/communist, worst of all.[17]

---

16. The most important source being Hannah Arendt, *The Origins of Totalitarianism* (New York: Harcourt, 1968).

17. The seminal article is Jeane J. Kirkpatrick, "Dictatorship and Double Standards," *Commentary* 78, no. 5 (November 1979). Kirkpatrick noted the tendency
of the left to gloss over the failings of Marxist regimes while drawing attention to
the human rights abuses of authoritarian regimes.

And in the context of an expansionist Soviet Union seeking to spread "revolution" throughout Asia, Africa, the Middle East, and Latin America, this rank order led to a distinctly neoconservative formulation of grand strategy for opposing communism: the United States, for moral reasons and not merely reasons of state, should try to prevent bad regimes from becoming worse regimes, which would thereby further enhance the strategic strength of the very worst regime, the Soviet Union. This policy would necessarily entail support for certain unsavory authoritarian governments in their efforts to combat local Communist insurrections (which, inevitably, traveled under the flag of national liberation movements). In its mature phase, the Reagan Doctrine[18] would entail providing military and other support for armed insurrections aimed at toppling Communist governments.

A detailed critique of the neoconservative view of foreign policy is beyond my scope here. As a second-generation neoconservative myself—one who can now look back from the vantage point of twenty or so years later upon my participation in the neoconservative intellectual scene during its (first) heyday—I would observe that the moralism of neoconservative foreign policy amounted to an overlay upon an essentially "realist" view of international relations. This "realist" grounding lent the project of reinvigorating anticommunism a tough-mindedness that I think was essential in confronting the view that Soviet communism presented no special problem in the world. But one must ask: How realistic—in the sense in which I have been praising the neoconservative reconnection with reality more broadly in this essay—was this grounding realism?

The "realist" school discounts what goes on within the borders of a country, including (from time to time) the stirrings of people for more freedom and better lives for themselves and their children. Although neoconservatives made a place in their analysis for heroic

18. First named and described by Charles Krauthammer in *Time* magazine (May 1, 1985).

individual dissent, in general, the tendency was to take totalitarian (if that term itself is not too abstract) *aspiration* for totalitarian *actuality*. The reality was substantially more complicated than theory might instruct. These countries all had *people* in them, and dividing them simply into two categories, oppressor apparatchik (the state) and hopeless victims (the people), did not do justice to the nuances nor to the possibility of dramatic change. Similarly, though in some cases the insurgents the Reagan Doctrine supported genuinely warranted the designation many neoconservatives applied to them rather broadly—namely, "freedom fighters"—in truth the practical test of the applicability of the term "freedom fighter" was often little more than the willingness to take up arms against Communist governments, not necessarily a commitment to anything like Western-style freedom.

But these retrospective assessments should not obscure either the importance of the classical neoconservative argument in its time or its legacy now. If one takes the argument's main line and merely updates it to take ensuing events into account, the result is quite striking. With the collapse of Soviet communism and, accordingly, of Marxist guerrilla movements operating here and there across the globe, one need no longer worry that authoritarian regimes, as a result of losing such struggles, will go from bad to worse. One is therefore under no moral obligation to provide support for these regimes. On the contrary, the full extent to which they are themselves morally suspect is now unobscured by the specter of something worse, and the authoritarian regimes can be judged accordingly: they are indeed wanting. From here, it is but a short step to support, in principle, universal liberalism—which, it will come as no great surprise, is the foreign-policy endpoint of our future politics.[19]

---

19. It is no accident that many of the leading neoconservative Cold Warriors, preeminently including Paul Wolfowitz, have emerged at the forefront of the Bush administration's efforts to promote the spread of liberalism and democracy in the Middle East. When Bush speaks in terms of a universal human entitlement to freedom, he is making claims similar to those here.

As it happens, the story is more complicated than that. After all, a worse outcome than an authoritarian regime is certainly possible in some cases. For example, holding an election might result in empowering an Islamist government bent on smothering all liberal sentiment under a blanket of *sharia*. Or an authoritarian government, under pressure to liberalize, might lose its grip altogether, resulting in a failed state prone to lawlessness, warlordism, and misery.

But, of course, to say this is merely to observe that one must be prudent in pursuit of the advance of liberalism—one must be realistic and take local circumstances fully into account; one must be attuned to the difficulty of introducing a balance between the desire for freedom and the desire for equality in places that have little or no experience of the two in relation and may not, in any event, wish this liberalism for themselves. One must not shrink from rejecting such illiberal wishes: Universal liberalism means nothing if it grants exceptions in principle—though, clearly, certain prudential accommodations may be necessary. In the end, however, it is the resolution of disagreement as "agreement to disagree" that most securely protects liberalism. This is no less true in the international context than in the domestic context (and, in my view, provides the only adequate account of the "democratic peace"[20]). If, at home, the politics of the future consists of the conservation of liberalism, abroad the same tendency—whether one wishes to call it "neoconservative" or something else—consists of the prudent promotion of liberalism.

Defending Liberalism Where It Is

Were the Soviet Union still an actor on the world stage, the possibility of universal liberalism might yet be concealed by the "realist" understanding of a bipolar world order and the reality of proxy conflict

---

20. I have developed this point at greater length in "The Atlanticist Community" in *Beyond Paradise and Power: Europeans, Americans and the Future of a Troubled Partenership*, ed. Tod Lindberg (New York: Routledge, 2004).

with the nuclear-armed USSR. One might find oneself content with a truncated vision of the possibility of liberalism—namely, with its flourishing in one's own political community but not, perhaps, elsewhere.

Neoconservatism generally shared in this sense of American exceptionalism. In the first place, the neoconservative intellectuals truly did feel "at home" in America. To the extent that a sense of alienation or critical distance from American society or government was a characteristic of previous generations of intellectuals, the neoconservatives well and truly repudiated it.[21] They were unabashed partisans of the American side because they thought the United States best embodied (*did* embody) the ideals for which they stood: liberty, equality of opportunity,[22] and so on. Moreover, they believed the United States had a unique role to play in the protection of and (to the extent possible) the spread of freedom on account of its position as a global power. This had been true throughout the twentieth century and remained true through the years of "superpower rivalry" (a term that risked a bristling response from neoconservatives because of its unstated premise—namely, the supposed "moral equivalence" of the two superpowers). The ability of the United States to project power

21. See *Our Country and Our Culture* (New York: Orwell Press, 1983). The volume is edited proceedings of a conference of the Committee for the Free World.

22. Neoconservatives liked to distinguish between the desire for equality of opportunity, which they favored, and the desire for equality of results, which they opposed, citing natural differences between people and the deleterious effects of attempting to redress them by redistributionist or other means. I agree with the latter proposition, and though I have previously made arguments in favor of "equality of opportunity," I am no longer able to say I know what the term means. Clearly, it begins with formal equality, in the sense that any little boy or girl can grow up to be president. But equally clearly, it does not end there. It has content, too, in the sense that we feel obliged to *create* opportunities for those who are in one way or another disadvantaged. I have described this above as the rebalancing of the desire for freedom and the desire for equality over time, pointing toward an end-state whose content we cannot know but that can be defined formally as "as much freedom as is consistent with equality," where equality is the mutual recognition of freedom.

in support of freedom was subject to practical constraint in the form of Soviet power. But to neoconservatives, the power the United States possessed was not in itself problematic, in the sense of Lord Acton's "power corrupts" or in any other sense, but rather something close to an unmixed blessing.

But what was specifically American about this "exceptionalism"? And how satisfactory, finally, was a satisfaction that stopped at the borders of the political community in question?

As for the Americanness of the exceptionalism, it was clearly rooted in the strong attachment in the United States to liberal democratic principles and the market economy, as well as the ability of the United States to defend those principles against all comers—and, more broadly, to defend the security of the free world. This Americanness stood in contrast not only to the Communist world but also, in certain respects, to the rest of the free world. The perceived deficiencies abroad were various, from socialist economic policies said to have brought on stagnation to the tenuousness of democracy to the very fact that the rest of the free world could not (and perhaps would not try to) defend itself in the absence of the United States. One could say that this exceptionalism pitted an idealized vision of the United States against (sometimes somewhat tendentiously described) realities elsewhere in order to declare reality abroad deficient by comparison.[23] In my view, however, it is not the exceptionalism that is the problem: Properly understood, this exceptionalism is nothing more or less than our universal liberalism. The problem is the identification of this exceptionalism as specifically "American," as if it were somehow confined to the United States. To be sure, the United States has played an important role historically as an exemplar and promoter of this liberalism and occupies the uniquely complicated position of

23. Similarly, Habermas and Derrida have recently created an idealized vision of "Europe" by which to judge the United States wanting. Jürgen Haberman and Jacques Derrida, "Plaidoyer pour un politique extérieure commune," *Liberation* (May 31–June 1, 2003).

liberal superpower (in which the tensions between power, as such, and liberalism emerge most fully, and often painfully[24]). It would also be empty to speak of liberalism as *prior to* its embodiment in states capable of defending themselves against illiberal forces at home or abroad. Nevertheless, when the United States promotes and defends its liberalism as its own, it is also promoting and defending the liberalism of others, of which liberalism in America is a part. Our current liberalism and our future liberal politics are not the sole property of Americans, even if the United States has played and continues to play a special role in their protection and extension. On the contrary, these things in principle belong to everyone—albeit, in actuality, not yet.

Especially from within a privileged political community, it is certainly possible to construct a defense of one's privileges: given a world in which good things are unevenly distributed, it is better to have the greater rather than the lesser share. This becomes an easier defense to make to the extent that one can attribute one's privileges to one's own superior internal arrangements rather than to the willful deprivation of others of some of what is rightly theirs. Moreover, there may well be reasons of force majeure mitigating in favor of such a defense—for example, the other's nuclear arsenal or perhaps its insistence on the destruction of our liberalism and replacement by something else.

But before long, and especially as circumstances change, the satisfaction such a defense provides begins to seem partial in character. This is because it is an illiberal defense of liberalism, a particular defense of something whose constitutive characteristics, the balancing of the fraternal desires for freedom and equality, can only be construed as fulfilled when universal. At a minimum, the universality must be incorporated into the particular defense in the acknowledgment that the defense is only contingently particular. At the same time, one

24. For a compelling description of this tension, see Peter Berkowitz, "Liberalism and Power," in Lindberg, ed., *Beyond Paradise and Power.*

must question the legitimacy of attempts to step outside the liberal community and criticize it *because* it is particular—that is, not universal. What follows from such a critique? Should one abandon liberalism where it is because it is particular? Surely not. Rather, what follows is that one should defend liberalism where it is and seek its extension. This proposition, however, is not a critique of liberalism but rather the essence of our current and future politics in support of liberalism.

There is no liberal standpoint outside liberalism. To be liberal is to have liberal relations with other liberals—mutual recognition of the freedom and equality of each in relation to the other.

In Conclusion

I have tried to show what I take to be the four most important ways in which the intellectual history of neoconservatism served as a precursor or progenitor of the future politics I have derived from liberalism's universal aspiration. The first of these, methodological in character, was the overriding new concern with the relationship between the ideal and the actual. The second was the discovery of the self-perpetuating qualities of liberal economic order, which in turn implies self-perpetuating qualities of the liberal social order that precedes it.[25] The third was the liberal case, in principle, for the universal extension of liberalism beyond its current boundaries. The fourth was the obligation to defend liberalism where it is even though it is not yet universal.

There are many other currents in the intellectual history of neoconservatism. Some of them, I readily grant, do not fit especially well

---

25. The liberal order is self-perpetuating in that its continuation requires nothing external to itself. But this is not to say that any given liberal order is necessarily permanent. It is subject to its own conservation, which, as I have discussed, entails balancing and rebalancing as necessary the desire for freedom and the desire for equality.

with what I have been describing. Many of these turn on questions of recognition of difference. For example, neoconservatives from the early days were sharply critical of gay rights and affirmative action, among other issues in "identity politics." The neoconservative arguments of the day, in many cases, had a distinctly illiberal cast. But these currents of neoconservatism, even if we find them wanting today, were not entirely out of keeping with what I have been talking about here. The neoconservative case against gay rights, for example, was chiefly based on the supposedly deleterious social consequences that would attend widespread acceptance of homosexuality. Insofar as homosexuality has become more widely accepted and the warned-of deleterious consequences have not come about, one could say that the neoconservative warnings were wrong. One could also say, however, that in subjecting the issue to empirical test, the neoconservative position left open the door to its potential reversal as evidence came in.

There is, then, a further connection between the neoconservative tradition and neoconservatism as the conservation of liberalism, as I have been describing. One could say that the neoconservatives, too, though they might not have put it that way, found themselves engaged in an effort across a variety of subjects to strike a balance between the desire for freedom and the desire for equality. This may have taken the form of seizing on perceived threats to the social order and sounding an alarm. And in some instances, they (I should say "we") may have been wrong about the threat. But in many instances, and arguably the most important, they/we were closer to right.

This, in turn, invites another question about what I have been calling our current and future politics. Where did it come from? I have traced here some influences through neoconservatism, but what else can we say about the *history* of the politics of the future?

In a certain respect, this politics is as old as liberalism itself. I do not mean to suggest that the illiberal opponents of the spread of liberalism were practitioners. However, from the moment that liberals themselves first had the thought that the advance of liberalism was not unproblematic—that scrupulous attention had to be paid to the reality of the here and now lest liberalism misstrike the balance between the desire for freedom and the desire for equality, and so jeopardize the project of its advance—from that moment on, we have had our politics of the future. In this respect, the neoconservatives were indeed practitioners, and not the first.

Nevertheless, one can hardly say that this politics of the future, the conservation and extension of liberalism, was born conscious of itself as such. That seems to have required a certain real-world progress of liberalism, the balanced expansion of the desire for freedom and the desire for equality, the acceptance of human difference on the basis of the mutual recognition of the freedom of each in the context of the equality of all in their freedom, the diminished sphere of the political in the sense of the resolution of disagreement into agreement to disagree. But by now, we have surely seen enough to know where we are going and—in formal terms at least, namely, the need for balance between the fraternal desires of liberalism, those for freedom and equality—what it will take to get there.

Varieties of Progressivism in America
Edited by Peter Berkowitz

Whereas conservatives in America often disagree over which moral
and political goods are most urgently in need of conservation,
contemporary progressives are principally divided over the means—
the kinds of government action—for achieving the progressive ends
around which they unite. *Varieties of Progressivism in America* focuses
on the debates within the party of progress about how best to
increase opportunity in America and to make social and political life
more egalitarian.

The contributors to this volume, offering different expertise and
different perspectives, combine varying voices, terminology, and
views of American politics to provide a better sense of the different
meanings of progressivism in our nation today. They examine the
Old Democrats of the New Deal, the contributions of the Clinton-era
New Democrats, and the future of progressivism in America.

Peter Berkowitz teaches at George Mason University School of Law
and is a fellow at the Hoover Institution. He is the author of two
books and the editor of several, including the companion to this
volume, *Varieties of Conservatism in America.*

Contributors: David Cole, Thomas Byrne Edsall, Franklin Foer,
William A. Galston, Jeffrey C. Isaac, Ruy Teixeira

Still, Muller failed miserably at the task of dividing the neoconservatives from the social conservatives. Abortion was not the issue to use, for opposition to abortion is, in fact, the defining feature of anything that shows the conservative impulse today. Not only does the new fusionism between social conservatives and neoconservatives suggest that this is so, but also a general shift seems apparent among the neoconservatives. Those who were mildly pro-abortion are now less so; those who were mildly anti-abortion are now extremely so.

What's more, opposition to abortion ought to be the definition of conservatism. If the American founding actually did preserve something, if there were any Edenist impulses in the Revolution that looked to allow the True Man to stand forth, then the slaughter of the innocents is the great betrayal of the platonic ideal of the United States. Here is the new fusionism to which the Right ought to look. Conservatives are those who refuse to forget what the American social order is an answer to. As they get off the radical modern train, at station after station, they will find this fact uniting them, and they will discover that many other divisions—not all, but many—can be put aside for the sake of life.

Libertarianism